CULTURE SMART!
CHINA

Kathy Flower

·K·U·P·E·R·A·R·D·

This book is available for special discounts for bulk purchases for sales promotions or premiums. Special editions, including personalized covers, excerpts of existing books, and corporate imprints, can be created in large quantities for special needs.

For more information contact Kuperard publishers at the address below.

ISBN 978 1 85733 502 6
This book is also available as an e-book: eISBN 978 1 85733 541 5

British Library Cataloguing in Publication Data
A CIP catalogue entry for this book is available from the British Library

First published in Great Britain
by Kuperard, an imprint of Bravo Ltd
59 Hutton Grove, London N12 8DS
Tel: +44 (0) 20 8446 2440 Fax: +44 (0) 20 8446 2441
www.culturesmart.co.uk
Inquiries: sales@kuperard.co.uk

Series Editor Geoffrey Chesler
Design Bobby Birchall

Printed in Malaysia

About the Author

KATHY FLOWER is a radio and TV producer, writer, and trainer who has specialized in the teaching of English as a Foreign Language. After leaving Paris, where she worked with the British Council, she went to Beijing from 1981 to 1983 and co-presented China's first major English language teaching series, "Follow Me," on Chinese TV. The series ran every night for six years and she is still known to hundreds of millions of viewers as *laoshi*, or "teacher." She has been back to work in China many times since. She runs an independent radio production company and lives in Sussex and southern France.

The Culture Smart! series is continuing to expand.
For further information and latest titles visit
www.culturesmart.co.uk

The publishers would like to thank **CultureSmart!**Consulting for its help in researching and developing the concept for this series.

CultureSmart!Consulting creates tailor-made seminars and consultancy programs to meet a wide range of corporate, public-sector, and individual needs. Whether delivering courses on multicultural team building in the USA, preparing Chinese engineers for a posting in Europe, training call-center staff in India, or raising the awareness of police forces to the needs of diverse ethnic communities, it provides essential, practical, and powerful skills worldwide to an increasingly international workforce.

For details, visit www.culturesmartconsulting.com

CultureSmart!Consulting and **CultureSmart!** guides have both contributed to and featured regularly in the weekly travel program "Fast Track" on BBC World TV.

contents

contents

Map of China

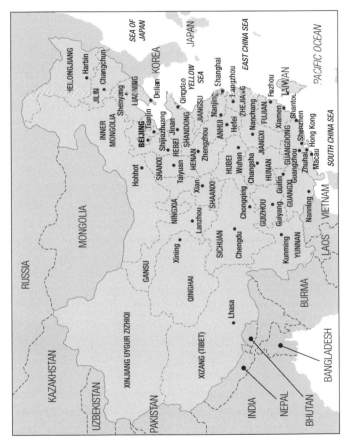

introduction

In the 1980s, I was invited to dinner at a Chinese friend's tiny, concrete floored apartment. Her mother-in-law came in to inspect me, the strange foreign creature. She asked, rather scornfully, if we had rice in the West and if we had tea. Then, triumphantly, she pointed to her tiny bound feet, inflicted on her when she was seven years old in a small provincial town in the 1930s. "Well, I bet you don't have *those* in the West," she said, very proudly, and hobbled off to make the dinner. That old lady's daughter-in-law became a fluent English-speaking university professor; and her grandson works for a Western company and funded his own studies at London University. It is the story of modern-day China in a nutshell.

For thousands of years, the Chinese believed that they had created a perfect social system. Dynasties came and went, but "Chineseness" remained essentially unchanged until the twentieth century. Following invasion by the Japanese, civil war, and revolution, on October 1, 1949, Mao Zedong and the Communists took power. Until Mao's death in 1976, China was largely closed off from the rest of the world, undergoing almost constant revolution at an often terrible price. When Mao died, the country cautiously opened its doors to the West and introduced a nascent market economy, called "socialism with Chinese characteristics." China became the "workshop of the world." Low wages and a low *yuan* boosted exports and gave jobs to millions, albeit on tiny salaries. China's status as an aspiring superpower was confirmed when it hosted the Olympic Games in 2008.

Soon after the spectacular Beijing Olympics, the world plunged into economic crisis. In China, too, factories closed, but most unemployed migrant workers made their way back to the countryside or tried their luck elsewhere. The government encouraged consumers at home to take the place of cash-strapped foreign buyers, with some success. The infinite patience and natural optimism that are part of the Chinese character has helped tide China over this bumpy patch. One thing, though, is sure: China can never again survive in splendid isolation from the rest of the world.

The Chinese have always taken a long-term view of events. They are proud of their ancient civilization and their modern achievements. But this pride is no longer tainted by the paranoid and uninformed xenophobia of old. Among the young, educated urban elite there is an eagerness to discuss issues that were formerly "off limits." *Culture Smart! China* aims to put all these changes into an historical context, explain deep-seated cultural attitudes, and guide the visitor through the maze of unfamiliar social situations. We hope it will enable you to discover for yourself the warmth, the intelligence, and the potential of the Chinese people.

I would like to dedicate this book to my friends in China. KF

Key Facts

Official Name	The People's Republic of China (PRC); in Mandarin, *Zhonghua Renmin Gonghe Guo*	The island of Taiwan (which has its own government) is called the Republic of China.
Capital City	Beijing (Peking)	
Main Cities	Chongqing (Chungking), Shenyang (Mukden), Wuhan, Nanjing (Nanking), Harbin	Major ports: Tianjin (Tientsin), Shanghai, Qingdao (Tsingtao), Guangzhou (Canton)
Area	3,695,500 sq.miles (9,571,300 sq. km.)	China is the third-largest country in the world.
Terrain	Range of types. Mountains, deserts, and arid basins in the north and northwest. Mountainous in the south. Rolling hills and plains in the east.	Two thirds of China is mountain or desert. The low-lying east is irrigated by the rivers Huang He (Yellow River), Chang Jiang (Yangtze-Kiang), and Xi Jiang (Si Kiang).
Climate	Temperatures vary greatly in the arid north, with hot summers and very cold dry winters. The south and east are warmer and more humid, with rainfall all year-round.	
Population	1.26 billion	The world's most populous country. Approx. one in four people live in China.

Population Density	Shanghai has 7,000 people per sq. mile; Beijing 1,927 per sq. mile; Tibet, only 5 people per sq. mile.	Most people live in the eastern central region, in the fertile flood plains.
Urban/Rural Divide	Approx. 382.3 million people live in urban areas, 877.2 million in rural areas.	The wealth gap between the cities and the countryside is enormous – among the highest in the world.
Ethnic Makeup	Approx. 93% Han Chinese; the rest are made up of "national minorities."	The non-Han are small in number, but concentrated in the border regions, and thus politically important.
Age Structure	0–15 yrs: 20.3% 15–29 yrs: 22.8% 30–44 yrs: 26.7% 45–59 yrs: 18.2%	60–74 yrs: 9.4% 75–84 yrs: 2.3% 85 and over: 0.3% (2007 figs.)
Life Expectancy	70 (m); 75 (f)	
Adult Literacy Rate	90.9% (2000 census)	
Languages	Mandarin (official), Cantonese, Wu, and others. There are seven main Chinese languages. All share the same script. Also other minority languages	
Religion	Officially atheist. Traditionally Daoist, Confucian, and Buddhist	Minority religious groups: Muslim, Catholic, and Protestant

culture smart! china

Government	Communist republic. Ruled by the Communist Party since 1949. There are other parties, but no general elections on the Western model.	
Economy	Moving from a centrally planned economy to a free market one. State-run enterprises are being replaced by market oriented factories.	Low wages in China mean it is used as the workshop of the world by richer industrialized nations.
Currency	*Renminbi*, or "people's money." Also known as *yuan* (dollar). 1 *renminbi* (*yuan*)=10 *jiao*=100 *fen*. There are 1, 5, 10, 50, and 100 *yuan* notes.	In transition from a "soft" to a "hard" currency. Approx 8 RMB to the US $; approx. 12 RMB to the UK £ (2002 rates)
Resources	Very many, and more waiting to be exploited. Oil in the South China Sea and in the northwest; vast mineral reserves. Forests in the south	
Agriculture	No longer self-sufficient in food. China has to feed almost a quarter of the world's population from the food it can produce on 15–20% of its land as the rest is not arable.	
Growth Rate	GDP is growing at an estimated rate of 8%, making China the best-performing market in Asia.	
Main Exports	Manufactured goods, including textiles, garments, electronics, arms	
Electricity	220 volts, 50 Hz. Standard wall sockets have three connectors. There are voltage adaptors in hotels, but it is advisable to bring your own.	

Media: Traditional	State-controlled and subject to censorship, but increasingly independent. *Renmin Ribao* (*People's Daily*) is the official Party newspaper. Chinese Central TV (CCTV) is the state broadcaster, with 16 national channels. Also about 300 regional TV and radio stations, and increasing numbers of foreign broadcasters. There are over 2,000 newspapers, 8,000 magazines, and 566 publishing houses.
Media: English Language	CCTV broadcasts in English and other foreign languages. There is an active (state-run) English-language press in China. *China Daily* is published six days a week, with a *Business Weekly* on Sunday. In Shanghai, the same company publishes the *Shanghai Star*. There are also magazines that list events, etc., aimed at the foreign community.
Media: New	Internet use in China is now a staggering 384,000,000 people, though this still is a mere 28.7% of the population (2009 figures).	There are thousands of Chinese-language Web sites, and every Chinese organization has one or plans to set one up. E-commerce is expected to grow.
Video/TV	China uses the PAL system. 96% of households have access to TV.	Videos using the American NTSC system will not work.
Internet Domain	.cn	
Telephone	International country code: 00 86	
Time Difference	GMT + 8 hrs	Although China extends across five time zones, Beijing time is used.

LAND & PEOPLE

TERRAIN AND CLIMATE

The People's Republic of China is vast. It has a total landmass of 3.7 million square miles (9.6 million sq. km), next in size only to Russia and Canada. At its maximum, it measures approximately 3,100 miles (5,000 km) north–south, and 3,230 miles (5,200 km) east–west. Its land border is 14,168 miles (22,800 km) long. Apart from the mainland, there are more than 5,400 islands, some just bare rocks that only appear at low tide.

Technically speaking, it encompasses five time zones, going east to west. However, despite the great distance of about 3,000 miles (4,828 km), the central Asian region of Xinjiang is on the same time zone as Beijing—which means that in Xinjiang it is still pitch dark at 10 o'clock in the morning.

Most of the rivers flow from west to east into the Pacific Ocean. The Yangtze River (Chang Jiang) is the longest at 3,915 miles (6,300 km)— and third longest in the world after the Nile and the Amazon—followed by the Yellow River

(Huang He) at 3,395 miles (5,464 km), the birthplace of Chinese civilization. However, in recent years, the Yellow River has been shortened by several hundred miles for months on end due to drying up near its delta. China's largest freshwater lake is Lake Poyang in the central Jiangxi province, with an area of 1,384 square miles (3,585 sq. km), and the largest salt lake is Lake Qinghai in the far west with an area of 1,769 square miles (4,583 sq. km).

China is a land of geographical and climatic extremes, and temperatures vary widely. Some parts are located in tropical and subtropical zones, while the north is in the frigid zone. In the south, vegetation remains green all year-round. The south and southwest have a much more agreeable climate, with lush green vegetation and beautiful wooded mountains wreathed in mists. The southwest is  the home of bamboo forests and that symbol of China, the panda; also of many plants familiar in the West, such as rhododendrons, which were brought to Europe by nineteenth-century botanists. The coastal regions are warm and humid, with four distinct seasons. In northern China, summers are hot and short, and winters long and cold. The humidity in the summer months is uncomfortably high— 60 percent—and in the winter the lack of moisture is almost painful, as humidity goes down to around 2 percent, leading to respiratory problems compounded by pollution and the dust from the nearby Gobi Desert.

To the north of the capital, Beijing, lie the huge empty grasslands of the Inner Mongolian Plateau. Mongolia is bitterly cold in winter, sometimes minus 40°F (minus 40°C), but it is a very dry and exhilarating cold with many fine, sunny days.

The world's highest mountain, Qomolangma Feng, better known in the West as Mount Everest, forms China's western border. It is part of the Himalayan range of mountains, forty of whose peaks rise to over 22,900 feet (7,000 m). In the northwest is the Tarim Basin, the largest inland basin in the world.

To the east of the Tarim Basin is the low-lying Turpan depression, called the "Oasis of Fire." This is the hottest place in China, with temperatures of up to 120°F (49°C) in summer. Xinjiang, where Turkic-speaking peoples live, is also home to the Taklamakan Desert, the largest in China.

Only about 15 percent of the terrain is suitable for agriculture. However, China is rich in natural resources, many of which are still waiting to be exploited. The oasis towns of the vast empty desert areas used to be rich because they were used for two thousand years as stopovers on the Silk Route—from the time of the Romans, caravans of camels would carry silk to the West. Salt from China's largest salt lake, Lop Nur, also went this way. Whoever controlled the oases could tax this traffic, so despite its arid deserts, Xinjiang was an attractive prize. Nowadays its prospects are even more attractive, as large oilfields are being developed by the central government, though not to the benefit of the locals.

So much of China is almost uninhabitable that, despite its huge size, around 90 percent of the people, mainly Han Chinese, are squeezed into about half of the area. The government is trying to resettle people in more sparsely populated areas, such as Tibet and Xinjiang in the far west, but the Han do not really want to live there (they consider places like Tibet barbaric and backward), and the locals are even less keen to have them, as the protests against Chinese rule over Tibet shortly before the 2008 Olympics showed. The majority of the Han population has for centuries lived mainly on the fertile flood plains at the lower reaches of the Yellow River and the Yangtze River. These two rivers deposit silt, which makes the flood plain the richest agricultural area in China. This is where the main cities have grown up, along with the key industries.

CHINA: A BRIEF HISTORY

The floodplains of the east were the cradle of Chinese civilization. Three thousand years ago, the Chinese were weaving silk, carving jade, casting bronze, and producing other alloys; creating sophisticated pottery, growing wheat, millet, and rice; and recording events using a written language of thousands of characters. The crossbow, used in Europe in the Middle Ages, was invented in China some fifteen centuries earlier. A thousand years before the English Industrial Revolution, China had advanced coke ovens and steel blast furnaces.

Chinese science, transmitted to Europe in waves, laid the foundation for many of the constituents of the modern world, while Chinese art, architecture, language, literature, and philosophy continue to be studied and admired by cultured people everywhere.

The Chinese speak with pride of their five thousand years of history, but in fact it goes back even further. Archaeologists have found evidence of Neolithic sites dating from before 5000 BCE. The earliest-known dynasty was the Xia, which ruled about 1994–1523 BCE. By the time of the Shang (or Yin) dynasty, which flourished in the Yellow River valley in 1523–1027 BCE, a sophisticated culture had developed, with an advanced bronze-manufacturing technology, a written language, and the first Chinese calendar.

The Mandate of Heaven

The last Shang ruler was a tyrant who was overthrown by the founders of the Zhou (or Chou) dynasty (1027–255 BCE). This period—which saw the introduction of money, iron, written laws, and the ethical philosophy of Confucianism— gave birth to the idea of the "Mandate of Heaven" (*Ti'en Ming*), in which Heaven gives wise rulers a mandate to rule, but takes it away from evil and corrupt ones. The Emperor became known as the

"Son of Heaven," a concept that still had potency right up until Mao Zedong's death in 1976. Later, the "Mandate of Heaven" began to incorporate the Daoist belief that Heaven sends natural disasters such as earthquakes and floods to show its disapproval of bad rulers.

During the Zhou period the Chinese people's sense of their unique identity and cultural superiority developed. The name *Zhong Guo*, or "Middle Kingdom," was coined to describe the central importance of China: anyone outside it was considered to be a barbarian. *Zhong Guo* is still the name used for modern China, while foreigners are referred to as *waiguoren*, literally, "[from] outside [our] country people." You may also hear the term *yang gweize*, literally "foreign devils," but it is more usually a term of joking endearment these days, like the Cantonese word "*gweilo*" used in Hong Kong to describe foreigners.

A time of war and turmoil followed, called the Warring States period (c. 500–221 BCE), in which the Zhou empire broke up into small kingdoms.

The moral philosopher Confucius wrote that the Zhou empire had been a golden age, and for centuries afterward, the Chinese would tend to look back to this as an idealized time.

The Qin (pronounced "Chin") dynasty (255–206 BCE) defeated its rivals and united the warring feudal states into a single empire. They introduced centralized government—standardizing weights and measures, writing systems, and money—and built a network of roads that joined the capital (near modern-day Xi'an) to the distant outposts of empire. The Emperor Shi Huangdi used thousands of slaves to build the Great Wall, which was designed to keep out the "Mongol hordes." The wall is largely destroyed now, but its remains can still be seen, stretching 4,000 miles (6,437 km) across the bleak northern plains of China. The last Qin emperor was Qin Shi Huang; his grave is famous worldwide, attracting crowds of tourists to see the terracotta army that stands guard over him.

During the Han dynasty (206–220 CE) the empire expanded into central Asia and was further centralized and effectively administered. The position of the Emperor changed from that of sole and absolute ruler to one in which power was delegated to a highly developed civil service. A complicated examination system, based on the candidates' knowledge of Confucianism, was set up to select people to work as bureaucrats; it lasted more or less unchanged for two thousand years. The Chinese people refer to themselves as the Han, and *hanyu* is one of the names for the Chinese language. During this period, Buddhism was introduced from India. Eventually a large-scale rebellion destroyed the Han, and the empire split into three competing kingdoms, resulting in the eventual victory of the Wei over the Chou and Wu. Confucianism was

superseded by Buddhism and Daoism; and
barbarian (Hun) invasions started in the north.
The Sui dynasty(581–618) reunified China,
halted the Huns, and repaired and strengthened
the Great Wall.

A Golden Age

The Sui were soon replaced by the Tang dynasty
(618–906). This really was a golden age for the
arts and for the country's prosperity. The Tang
capital was in what is now Xian; called
Chang'an, it was one of the world's greatest
cities, rivaling Rome and Constantinople, with a
population of one million inside the walls, and a
society with many modern features such as
commerce, tax collection, civil administration,
tolerance of different religions, and a thriving
culture. It was especially famous for its poetry
and pottery. The Tang continued the building of
canals that linked different parts of the empire,
and they built inns for traveling officials,
merchants, and pilgrims to break their journeys.
There were more contacts with foreigners than
at any other time until the twentieth century.
The Tang provided a model for the later
Song, Ming, and Qing dynasties.

The Tang empire disintegrated
into the "Five Dynasties and
Ten Kingdoms" amid war
and economic decline.
Nevertheless, this period saw
the development of printing.

The Song dynasty (960–1279) reunified China and restored order. This was a period of calm and creativity. However, the frontiers were neglected, and Mongol incursions began.

Despite the Middle Kingdom's best attempts to seal itself off from the outside world, foreigners continued to find their way in, sometimes as invaders, sometimes as ambassadors or merchants. The most famous traveler of all, the Venetian Marco Polo, visited China in 1275–92. He wrote the first real account of China, of its rich cities, bigger than any to be found in Europe, and of a well-ordered society.

Some Chinese "Firsts"

Engraved woodblock printing on paper and silk was invented in the seventh century; the world's oldest surviving printed book is a Chinese Buddhist text printed in 868 CE. Another Chinese first was the invention of moveable type in the eleventh century.

By then, undeterred by the Great Wall, the Mongols had poured across the Gobi Desert on their ponies. They made Beijing their capital, and Kublai Khan became the first emperor of the Yuan dynasty (1260–1368). The Yuan were ruthless but efficient rulers; they improved the roads into China and Russia, promoted trade nationally and internationally, and even set up a famine relief system.

Widespread revolts drove out the Mongols, and the first emperor of the native Chinese Ming dynasty (1368–1644) that succeeded them was of poor peasant stock; there are echoes of Mao Zedong in the first Ming emperor's totalitarian rule, with its stifling of intellectual freedom and personal initiative. Mongolia was captured by the second Ming emperor. In another foretaste of Mao's attitudes, the Ming considered China as superior in every way, with nothing to learn from other cultures. Thus, while Europe was growing ever more dynamic and prosperous, China started to stagnate. However, there was architectural development and Beijing flourished as the new capital.

European Intervention

Foreigners not only came overland but also arrived by sea. The first European ships to land in China were from Portugal, then a great trading nation with imperial ambitions. The Portuguese arrived in 1516 and were allowed to set up a trading post in Macau. They were soon followed by the British, the Dutch, and the Spanish. The Ming were succeeded by another non-Chinese dynasty, the Qing (1644–1912), nomads from Manchuria, who like the others soon assimilated into Chinese culture.

The Qing government kept the foreigners as far away from them as possible, by making them stay in Canton (Guangzhou). But this did not prevent the start of a trade that was to become a byword for Western imperialism: the sale by the British of Indian-grown opium to the Chinese.

The Opium Trade

Although from a modern viewpoint selling opium in return for tea and silk seems no better than drug pushing, opium had been used for centuries for pain relief, as an early form of antidepressant, as a muscle relaxant, and to kill hunger pangs. People were aware of the risk of addiction to the drug, but its use was legal and quite widespread in many countries until the end of the nineteenth century.

Opium addiction increased rapidly in China, and the Emperor tried to ban the trade in 1800. But the British were at last getting plenty of tea, silk, and porcelain in exchange for their noxious product, and the Chinese middlemen were doing well too. The Emperor's decree was ignored. The opium trade continued unchecked until 1839, when the Chinese took unilateral action and seized 20,000 chests of opium. So began the first of the notorious Opium Wars (1839–42),

with the British attacking Canton; Britain forced China to cede Hong Kong and open five ports to European trade. There were to be another three of these wars in the nineteenth century, fought with Russian, French, and American support, and poisoning the Chinese view of Western "foreign devils" for the next hundred years.

By 1860 the West had won huge concessions: foreigners could settle in many different parts of China, exempt from Chinese laws, and the Chinese were forced to pay large war indemnities. As the nineteenth century drew to a close, the Throne of Heaven was occupied by a minor, the four-year-old Emperor Kuang Hsu, but real power lay in the hands of his aunt, the Dowager Empress Tzu Hsi, who, rather than move China forward into the industrial age, presided over its total disintegration.

The European imperial powers were attacking on all sides: in 1883 France took Vietnam, and eventually Laos and Cambodia, from China; the British took over Burma; Japan made a bid for Korea and Taiwan; and by 1898, Russia, Britain, France, and Germany were all set to carve up the rest of China between them. Partition was prevented just in time by the USA's proposal for an open-door policy instead of "spheres of influence."

The Boxer Rebellion

Worse was to come. The Dowager Empress raised taxes and added to the misery of the peasantry. War, floods, famine, and drought plagued the last years of the dying century, with the foreign powers profiting at China's expense. Peasant anger erupted in the Boxer Rebellion.

The anti-Western Society of the Harmonious Fist, popularly known as the Boxers, was born in Shangdong province and nurtured by the weakened Qing government, who saw their popularity with the peasantry as a chance to get the foreigners out of China and to hang on to power. The Boxers massacred foreign missionaries and Chinese Christians, destroyed churches and railway lines, and then, in 1900, marched to Beijing and attacked the foreign compounds. Rapid intervention by foreign troops meant that they lost this battle, but more and more secret societies were springing up all over China, aimed at toppling the Qing dynasty and getting rid of the foreign powers.

Dr. Sun Yat Sen, still revered as the father of modern China, became the leader of one of these

groups, the Guomindang (National People's Party) in 1905, and events started to move fast. The Dowager Empress died at last, in 1908, as did Kuang Hsu, and the two-year-old Pu Yi came to the throne—later to be immortalized in Bertolucci's film *The Last Emperor*. The little boy's reign was very brief. Revolution broke out in 1911. The Qing government finally acknowledged defeat, and in 1912 Sun Yat Sen proclaimed the Republic of China.

Warlords, Nationalists, and Communists
After the abdication of the infant Emperor, General Yuan Shih-Kai became dictator. On his death in

1916 effective central government collapsed. Internal feuding, extreme poverty, warlordism in the north, and lawlessness became rife, and Japan had not given up its imperial ambitions. In 1919 it was ceded Germany's Chinese possessions. In 1921 Sun Yat Sen was elected President of the nominal National Government. The same year saw the founding of the Chinese Communist Party, which had strong links with the new Soviet regime in neighboring Russia. From 1923 the Communists worked with the Guomindang to reunite China, and gradually won the support of the Chinese peasants. Sun Yat Sen died in 1925, and the new leader of the Guomindang, Chiang Kai Shek, declared war on the Communists, instead of uniting with them.

The civil war that began in 1926 ushered in terrible times: children worked in factories for twelve hours a day, people starved to death on the streets, and every night carts collected hundreds of corpses as though they were so much rubbish. While the Communists and the Guomindang fought each other for control of China, the Japanese overran Manchuria in 1932, setting up the puppet state of Manchukuo, and then in 1937 attacked Shanghai. During the Second World War the various political groups united against the  Japanese invaders. From 1941 Chiang Kai Shek received help from the USA and Britain.

In 1934–5 the Communists undertook the "Long March" from southeast to northwest China to escape encirclement by the Guomindang. Open civil war resumed in 1946, and in 1949 the Red Army led by Mao Zedong defeated the Nationalists at Nanjing. Chiang Kai Shek fled to the island of Formosa (now Taiwan), taking with him the entire gold reserves of his impoverished country. On October 1, 1949—now National Day and a public holiday—Mao Zedong declared the People's Republic of China a reality.

The People's Republic

For a while, daily life improved for most Chinese, and many look back on the beginning of the 1950s as the best period of Mao's rule. But in 1958 the "Great Leap Forward," the extremist five-year plan to accelerate the economy, marked the beginning of campaigns that were driven by ideology rather than economic pragmatism. As ever, natural disasters on a huge scale also played their part: floods and droughts in 1959 and 1960 ruined two harvests, and led to famine; and, worst of all, after the Sino-Soviet split in 1960 the Soviet Union stopped giving aid to China. Mao fell out of favor, and for a while, in the mid-1960s, Deng Xiao Ping (who would later become President) and Liu Shaoqi held power. Free markets were encouraged, the peasants were allowed to own their land, and the Soviet-influenced policies that had failed so disastrously were abandoned.

Permanent Revolution

Mao felt that China was slipping back into its old capitalist ways, and retaliated by unleashing the "Great Proletarian Cultural Revolution," whose shock troops were the Red Guards. Its aim was "to hold aloft the banner of Mao Zedong's thought . . . struggle against the capitalist roaders . . . and to transform education, literature, and art   to facilitate the development of the socialist system." From 1965 until Mao's death from Parkinson's disease on September 9, 1976, China was engulfed in cruelty and orchestrated chaos. Schools and universities closed, teachers were humiliated and persecuted; anyone labeled an intellectual or a capitalist could be tortured, killed, or sent to labor in atrocious conditions; the arts became an instrument of control, with bookshops selling Mao's *Little Red Book* of thoughts and very little else; the only music allowed was one of eight "Revolutionary Model Operas" that Mao's wife, Jiang

Qing, considered suitably proletarian. Millions died, many committing suicide in despair. It is almost impossible to reconcile this period of collective madness and brutality with today's vibrant, confident China—but it happened.

The Open Door Policy

Mao had, in fact, belatedly supported the efforts of Prime Minister Zhou Enlai to restore order in 1970.

A window of opportunity opened in 1972 with President Nixon's visit to China. After Mao's death, his wife Jiang Qing and the other members of the infamous "Gang of Four," were arrested. Deng Xiao Ping, supreme survivor against all the odds, returned to power in 1977. Deng's greatest achievement was the "Open Door Policy" that put China back into the global community on which it had for so long turned its back. Deng's famous statement that "It does not matter what color the cat is, so long as it catches mice" was the antithesis of Mao's rigid dogmatism. He introduced market incentives and encouraged foreign trade, and his pragmatic economic policies have been built on by his successors ever since.

After a century of trauma, the Chinese people are rebuilding civil society. Since 1979, China's economy has doubled roughly every seven-and-a-half years. The country is almost self-sufficient in food. Many more children have access to vaccines, clean drinking water, and basic health care. Life expectancy has increased.

Milestones at the end of the twentieth century were the terrible events in Tiananmen Square in 1989, which, though shocking, did not plunge China back into civil war as many had feared; and the surprisingly peaceful handover of the British-leased territory of Hong Kong back to Chinese rule in 1997, which, again contrary to expectations, did not result in Mao-style revenge attacks on outspoken journalists and politicians. The twenty-first century has already produced three more milestones: China's successful bid to host the Olympics in 2008; its unequivocal support for the US-led antiterrorism campaign; and, probably the most significant of all, its entry into the World Trade Organization in 2001, after fifteen long years of negotiations.

THE GROWTH OF NEW CITIES

China is the most populous country in the world. For thirty years after the founding of the PRC, couples were encouraged to produce more revolutionaries and the population doubled. "The more Chinese, the better," said Mao; so the traditional Chinese desire for big families went unchecked until 1979. Since then the government has tried by every possible means to enforce the highly unpopular One Child family policy. It has had much success in the cities among the educated middle classes, less so in the countryside where more than two-thirds of the people still live. Even by official Chinese estimates, 25 million babies are born each year, and in common with other rapidly industrializing countries, the Chinese are now living to a ripe old age, adding to the population burden at the other end of the scale.

The recent economic reforms have caused huge regional disparities and growing economic stratification. Approximately 2.8 million households had an annual income of 100,000 RMB in 2001, but the subsistence class, approximately 106.2 million households, had an annual income of 5–10,000 RMB. For the past thirty years the general economic trend has been an improvement in living standards. In 1978 there were 250 million people living in abject poverty, about 26 percent of the rural population. By 1994, this had been reduced to 80 million, and it is theoretically due to be halved again—if the fallout from the global crisis is not too bad. Despite official restrictions on taking up residence in the towns, every year millions of peasants leave impoverished parts of the countryside to find work in the cities. Partly because of the money they send home, many Chinese have become relatively prosperous in the past twenty years, and the World Bank estimates that by 2020 per capita income will be approaching Portugal's in the 1990s—though that is still less than half that of the United States.

In order to ease the pressure on the swelling cities, the Chinese government, as well as dispersing the population to other areas of the country, is building brand-new cities, one a week according to some reports. The number of cities with a population of more than 500,000 has increased from twelve to eighty-one. Beijing, Shanghai, and Chongqing are three of the most densely populated, with Shanghai clocking up a tremendous 7,000 people per square mile (2,700 per sq. km). By way of contrast, mountainous Tibet has just five people in the same amount of space. The eastern cities, though crowded, are wealthier and are better served by good schools, hospitals, and libraries than are the more remote areas. There are more shops, a much greater variety of goods, more culture, and far more opportunities both for native Chinese and for the foreign businessperson.

HAN CHINESE AND MINORITY NATIONALITIES

Ninety-two percent of the population of China are of the Han race, or what the West calls Chinese. Minority nationalities generally live in the northwestern and southwestern extremities of the country, and tend to stay there rather than move around and integrate with other ethnic groups. Fifty-five minority nationalities are officially recognized, totalling just over 100 million people. They have their own customs, languages, dress, and religions. Many in the northwest, near the borders with Pakistan, Afghanistan, India, and Russia, are Muslim. Tibetans, Mongolians, Lobas, Moinbas, Tus, and Yugurs are Lamaists. The Dai, Blang, and Deang people are Buddhists. A considerable number of the Miao, Yao, and Yi people are Christian. Official attitudes toward their different customs are a complex mixture of tolerance and control. They are exempted from the One Child policy, but the ancient Chinese belief in the superiority of Han Chinese culture is as strong as ever in regions like Tibet or Xinjiang.

Mandarin is promoted throughout China as the official spoken language of the country, and all minority peoples are urged to learn it. But the government has also helped to create written languages for ten minority nationalities, including the Zhuang, Bouyei, Miao, Dong, Hani, and Li, which prior to 1949 had only spoken languages.

Although the minority nationalities represent a comparatively small proportion of China's total population, they have a geopolitical importance far beyond their numbers because of the strategic territories they occupy along China's sparsely populated and porous frontiers.

GOVERNMENT AND POLITICS

Although often seen as a one-party state, China has eight "democratic parties," some of them formed more than fifty years ago, which have an advisory role to the Communist Party. The Communist Party of China was founded on July 1, 1921. Currently, it has more than 58 million members, with over 3.3 million grassroots branches. But membership is no longer a prerequisite for getting a good job. The State Council, which is the highest level of state administration in China, is the Central People's Government. Under this are a whole swathe of commissions, ministries, provincial governments, and corporations. The State Planning Commission and the State Commission for Restructuring the Economy coordinate policy at the national level. China is still a very slow and bureaucratic society, unused to the rapidity of decision making and the freedoms of North America and Western Europe, and of course the government is not democratically elected. But compared to the period right up to the late 1990s, when the dead hand of state interference blighted any attempt at doing business, or any individual initiative whatsoever, the period from the early 1990s until the global downturn in 2008 have been halcyon days for the go-ahead entrepreneur.

Political stability has increased, attempts have been made to root out official corruption, many unnecessary layers of government have been abolished, and a start has been made on developing the rule of law. This is potentially the biggest change of all, and means that the private citizen is theoretically able to take corrupt officials to court for the first time (though it is still far from easy to do), and also that foreign companies have at least nominal legal protection, thanks to the increasingly sophisticated system of commercial law. Individual Chinese organizations can now have access to foreign currency, and can make their own arrangements to meet foreign partners, produce or market a product, or travel abroad. As with most developing nations moving from a centrally planned to a market economy, the closure of inefficient state enterprises has brought unemployment, poverty, and social unrest, but, at least until the global recession began, new market oriented businesses have been able to move in to take up the slack.

The price of China's membership of the World Trade Organization, the subject of years of protracted negotiations, was that it had to agree to open scrutiny of legal processes, to cutting import tariffs, to applying international safety and inspection measures, and to putting an end to the piracy of other countries' products, which is rife at present. Some companies in China are worried that the price is too high, but in the (very) long term, membership of the WTO should help to strengthen the rule of law and the country's stability and prosperity.

THORNY ISSUES: THE MEDIA, FREE SPEECH, AND HUMAN RIGHTS

There are still some taboos when it comes to conversation with ordinary Chinese people— the "three 'T's" for example, Tibet, Taiwan, and Tienanmen Square. Most Chinese are initially reticent about criticizing their country to a foreign visitor—as we all are perhaps—but once they know and trust the visitor, they will open up. Educated, English-speaking young people in particular enjoy discussions about world affairs and are extremely well informed. They are also much readier to question and debate than they once were, as the state education system has been trying to encourage creativity, not just rote learning.

The Media

The media in China is state controlled, but this simple statement belies the huge growth in the number of newspapers and magazines, as well as in independent radio and TV stations, and TV and radio from outside China. The sector is becoming more competitive and commercial, with pay-TV estimated to have 128 million subcsribers. But, in the words of the BBC's correspondent in China, "The opening-up of the media industry has extended to distribution and advertising, not to editorial content."

BBC News cited a classic example of state control over editorial content in January 2009—China's coverage of President Obama's inaugural address. An English-language version of the speech on the Web site of the state-run Xinhua news agency included these words from President Obama in full: "Recall that earlier generations faced down fascism and communism, not just with missiles and tanks, but with sturdy alliances and enduring convictions." But in the Chinese-language version, the word "communism" was taken out. President Obama's warning to world leaders who "blame their society's ills on the West" also vanished from the Chinese version; and when he went on to say "To those who cling to power through corruption and deceit and the silencing of dissent, know that you are on the wrong side of history," once again, Xinhua included the passage in full in its English version, but the sentence was taken out of the Chinese translation. China Central Television, the country's main broadcaster, aired the speech live with a simultaneous Chinese translation. But when the translator got to the part where President Obama talked about facing down communism, her voice suddenly faded away.

The program suddenly cut back to the studio, where a presenter was caught off guard.

Ordinary Chinese journalists and people working in the media are aware of the almost clumsy stupidity of treating the Chinese people like children in this way. But they have to live with it—for the time being. That is why, for safety's sake, TV news broadcasts are usually prerecorded, not live. News bulletins may still take several days (or weeks) to report on domestic disasters such as fires, floods, or industrial accidents, while dwelling on those in other countries (often by using film footage from those countries' own uncensored news programs), and they will still tend to concentrate on the heroic efforts of the People's Liberation Army to rescue flood victims rather than investigate whether the flood was caused by official mismanagement or environmental degradation. There may have been a huge growth in the quantity of TV channels, but it has not been matched by a growth in quality of programs. The visitor who idly switches on the TV in their hotel room is likely to be regaled with nonstop pop songs, mostly Chinese, as the pop industry is booming; romantic films, much sexier than anything that would have been allowed a few years ago, and lots of quizzes. What they will not see are hard-hitting documentaries or challenging interviews with politicians.

Newspapers and TV dare not champion individuals who have been wronged by the state, though they do routinely criticize official corruption. A few brave journalists have tried to get local TV and newspapers to run stories on scandals that any Western news editor would leap at, such as the abduction of children to work as slaves in a brick factory, or the collapse of a road bridge built with substandard concrete. But they are usually stopped by a web of officials involved with the very corruption that the stories are trying to expose. Only when stories are big enough to break through to the outside world, as with the notorious case of the baby milk adulterated with melamine in 2008, does the state media weigh in.

The often undisputed and misused power of local village officials over poor peasants is another cause of much human misery in remote rural areas, where few foreigners ever venture. Reforms passed in Beijing take time to reach the countryside. As a result, people's only recourse to "justice" is sometimes to take to the streets. Official Chinese figures recorded 87,000 such protests in 2005, or "mass incidents" as they are known in China. Visitors to Beijing's Forbidden City will often see crowds outside who are not mere sightseers. They are some of the hundreds of thousands of Chinese who travel to the capital every year to lodge petitions with the authorities for the righting of wrongs, such as being evicted from their land by developers greedy for real estate. All in all, China's economic reform has not been matched by political change and democracy is still a distant dream of a few dissidents. The ruling Communist party cracks down on dissenters and often sends them to labor camps. Torture is still routinely used on suspects, and protests by religious cults such as the banned Falun Gong, or by ethnic minorities such as the Tibetans and the Muslim Uighurs in the northwest, are harshly repressed.

Nonetheless, individual freedom in China has grown enormously, despite the many restrictions. The Internet, the increase in the number of Chinese who can and do travel abroad, and the huge growth in the number of overseas visitors coming into China (54 million in 2007) have had an enormous and positive impact, at least among the urban elite. China has the largest number of Web users in the world. It also has some of the tightest controls on sites of which it does not approve: try typing words like "freedom" or "Falun Gong" into a search engine while in China and watch it mysteriously crash. But there are usually ways round them, the Chinese being very savvy Internet users.

Books and Periodicals

In the late 1960s, as the youth of the Western world luxuriated in a miasma of free love and mind-bending drugs, Mao's mobs of Red Guards were invading private homes, schools, and universities, burning countless thousands of books and scrolls, bent on destroying any book other than the *Quotations From Chairman Mao*, better known in the West as the *Little Red Book*. Traditionally the Chinese have placed huge value on books and book learning, and nowadays they are again free to read virtually anything. Some books such as Jung Chang's highly critical biography of Mao (*Mao: The Unknown Story*) are still not sold openly, but the range of books both Chinese and foreign is vast. Go to the huge five-storey bookshop in Beijing's main shopping street, Wanfujing, and you will find a crowd of eager book buyers, from children who can barely toddle to newly retired workers hungry for self improvement. Imported books in English are expensive though, so take plenty to read before you leave home. English-language publications such as *China Daily* are state owned, censored, and therefore bland, but some independent ones such as *Time Out* are interesting and fun to read when you are in China.

THE ENVIRONMENT

The discerning reader will by now have realized that China is full of paradoxes; environmental issues are no exception to the rule. The bad news is that the environment is in trouble in China; the good news is that the government at least acknowledges that there are huge problems and allows outside agencies such as the World Bank in to monitor the situation. The Bank says that sixteen of the world's twenty most polluted cities are in China, which is also blamed for some of the air pollution in neighboring Japan and Korea. At the Copenhagen summit in 2010, China agreed to limit its

greenhouse gas emissions, and promised to reduce its use of fossil fuels by up to 45 percent. But China's booming economy has put it at the top of the league of CO_2 emitters, ahead of the USA. Eight of the world's ten most polluted cities are in China, and visitors will taste, smell, and see for themselves the results of burning millions of tons of black sulphurous coal, especially in the colder months. If you go to see the 1,500-year-old giant statues of Buddha carved in the Yungang caves, in the city of Datong, eight hours by train from Beijing, you'll also discover what it is like to live in a city dominated by the production and burning of coal. Datong has coal in the air, on people's faces, and on the grey laundry hung out to dry, just as many British mining towns did in the past. New technology may eventually reduce carbon emissions from the coal, but it is taking time.

The quantity and quality of water supplies are also worrying the authorities—rivers are drying up in the north, due to overuse of river water for energy and manufacturing, and in some areas flooding has got worse because too many buildings have been built on floodplains.

China's wildlife has also suffered from unregulated hunting and the destruction of habitat. The panda has become the international symbol of China's wildlife, and the high profile battle to save it has been largely successful. But lesser known animals have not fared as well. Many less-educated, poor Chinese regard animals solely as a source of food for humans. Some are unlucky enough to be valued for their medicinal properties. Ground-up tiger bones are used to enhance male potency, as are rhino horns and other strange ingredients. Visitors to the outdoor food markets in southern China will see many threatened species being sold alive, as this is a guarantee of freshness in a country where fridges are still rare. The sight of wild creatures such as musk deer, pangolins, raccoons, and tiny monkeys, cooped up in cramped, filthy cages waiting to be killed and cooked is very distressing. However, more than 300 nature reserves have been established, which protect over 1.8 percent of the land area. Many animals are, officially at least, protected. Illegal hunting and trapping continues, but in the battle between conservationists and poachers at least the conservationists have the law on their side. Another hopeful sign is that CCTV, China's national broadcast network, is now putting out programs about the environment that are an honest attempt to explore the problems and to reeducate a population who were told for decades of the benefits of heavy industry and relentless urbanization—while no mention was ever made of the costs.

HONG KONG, TAIWAN, AND MACAU

For many years, English-language maps printed in China showed Hong Kong with the letters "oc. GB" after its name, standing for "occupied by Great Britain." Hong Kong, along with Portuguese "occupied" Macau, is now safely back as part of the PRC. Taiwan (also known as the Republic of

China) still remains a sensitive issue for the Chinese. US law obliges the Americans to support Taiwan, but when they interpret the idea of support as more than just verbal, as in the offer early in 2010 to sell a large quantity of arms to Taiwan, the Chinese react furiously. Nonetheless, there are now direct flights between Taiwan and the mainland and a lot of business goes on—in both directions.

Taiwan

Taiwan has its own government and currency, but its sovereign status is ambiguous. The major world powers acknowledge China's claims to Taiwan, and only a handful of countries officially recognize it as a nation state. The politically dominant "mainlanders" and their descendants comprise 11 percent of the island's population and are still closely associated with Chiang Kai Shek's defeated Nationalists. The majority, the Taiwanese, are descendants of earlier Han Chinese immigrants, and there is a history of resentment of political dominance by the "mainlanders." There are also so-called "aboriginals," who speak languages belonging to the Austronesian family and have close cultural affinities with maritime Southeast Asia. Almost everybody in Taiwan subscribes to a fourfold division of the island's population—"Taiwanese" *(tai wan sheng)*, "Mainlanders" (*wai sheng jen*), "Hakka" (*k'o chia jen*), and aborigines (*shan ti jen*)—though this provides at best a rough-and-ready guide to the country's cultural complexities.

Hong Kong

Hong Kong has retained many of the traditions that were banned for years in the PRC, side by side with the tremendous vibrancy and the work ethic that have made it so successful economically. There is a relatively free press, too, and many of the fashions, songs, and "lifestyle choices" made by the inhabitants of Hong Kong are very attractive to the rest of China, especially the Cantonese-speaking south—Cantonese is the language of Hong Kong. Until the return of Hong Kong to China in 1997, illegal immigrants were stopped by the British police every day trying to cross over the wire fences of the border, or swim to the island through the shark-infested seas. Ironically enough, this is still going on—except that it is now the Chinese police who have the task of preventing poor Chinese migrants from coming to feast off the Hong Kong honeypot.

Macau

Macau was never as wealthy as Hong Kong, and therein lies much of its unspoiled charm. Luckily, in 2005 UNESCO gave the center of Macau World Heritage status. So despite many huge new, brash Las Vegas-style skyscrapers, tiny Macau has kept its wonderful blend of Chinese and Mediterranean influences, still visible in its colorful colonial-style buildings. When the British ruled Hong Kong, and the Portuguese ruled Macau, thousands of Hong Kong Chinese would take the ferry over to Macau every weekend to indulge their passion for gambling. Casinos were forbidden by the British, but the gamblers were free to do as they pleased in Macau, which welcomed the trade as it had little other source of income. Gambling, along with many other previously forbidden pleasures, has made a timid comeback in China, but Macau's casinos are noisier and busier than ever.

THE OVERSEAS CHINESE, AND CHINA'S INFLUENCE ON ITS NEIGHBORS

Historically, Chinese civilization had a strong influence on neighboring countries, notably Vietnam and Korea, and to a lesser extent Japan. The majority of Southeast Asian countries lay outside direct Chinese control, though many paid tribute to the emperor. However, pressure of population in China itself, plus invasions, civil wars, and economic problems, has meant that for centuries there has been a steady flow of people leaving China. The earliest emigrants were traders and craftsmen who moved to Southeast Asia, where they continue to play a dominant role in business throughout the region. These Chinese migrants may be divided into two groups: the "Straits" Chinese, who are the descendants of pre-nineteenth-century migrants; and the nineteenth- and twentieth-century migrants from South China: Cantonese, Teochew, Hakka, and Hokkein.

Later, in the nineteenth century, laborers or "coolies" (from the Chinese words *ku li*, or "bitter strength") were recruited in very large numbers from south China for work in British, French, and

Dutch colonies, and in the Americas. By the 1930s, there were nearly ten million overseas Chinese, and many of the descendants of those laborers still live in Chinese communities in their adopted countries today.

Traditionally, overseas Chinese have sent money back home to their families, and the very successful ones have invested in factories back in their homeland or endowed universities. Many workshops and factories in southern China are run by émigré Chinese from Hong Kong and Taiwan, but the working conditions in some of these factories are less than ideal. The attitude of the mainland Chinese to their overseas cousins is often a rather unpleasant mixture of resentment and grudging admiration, and it can be harder for such people to be accepted than for foreigners.

CHINESE SOUTHEAST ASIAN DIASPORA	
Indonesia	7.2m
Thailand	5.8m
Malaysia	5.2m
Myanmar	1.5m
Philippines	0.8m
Singapore	2.0m
Vietnam	0.8m
Rest of Asia & Australia	1.8m

(*Overseas Chinese Economy Yearbook*) (m = million)

VALUES & ATTITUDES

CHINESE PHILOSOPHY

The history of China has been built on social order (albeit not always combined with social justice), and that remains true to this day. As far as the Han Chinese are concerned, the four major cultural factors that have influenced the development of their society in the past three millennia are Confucianism, Legalism, Daoism, and Maoism/Marxism.

Confucianism

The ethical system first laid down by Confucius in the sixth century BCE emphasized personal virtue, promotion on merit by scholarship, devotion to the family, and justice. Mao Zedong may have elevated devotion to the "people" or State above the family, but the essentially conservative tenets of the sage are now being invoked by the Communist Party again in the interests of creating a more civilized, united nation. For contemporary Chinese, Confucianism has good and bad points. In representing the Chinese spirit and culture for so long, it is credited with helping the country survive numerous trials and difficulties, and its teachings are seen as compatible with the need for courtesy, justice, honesty, and honor. Others argue that Confucianism was the strongest bulwark of the monarchy and of feudalism, and hence is irrelevant today.

Legalism

The Legalists, who had their brief moment of glory at the time of the Qin emperor Shi Huangdi's reunification of the divided land in 211 BCE, had a less charitable view of human nature and of the potential for individuals to achieve social order on their own. To the Legalists, Man essentially was born sinful, and only the full force of arbitrary law ruthlessly applied could quell his baser impulses.

Daoism

The joyful, irreverent, quietist philosophy of Daoism, enunciated by the sage Lao Zi (born about 570 BCE), rejected both the moral idealism of Confucianism and the laws of Legalism as products of social contrivance, leading to hypocrisy or to exploitation. For the Daoists, justice flowed from living in a state of harmony with the natural world around us.

Marxism/Maoism

The writings of Karl Marx, which had such an influence on the nineteenth- and twentieth-

century revolutionaries, were rooted in the
rationalism of the Enlightenment and the morality
of the Judeo-Christian religious tradition. Dr. Sun
Yat Sen, as well as many of the early Chinese
revolutionaries, was also influenced by Christian
ideas of good and evil. Basic concepts of social
justice, the equality of all men, looking after the
poorest members of society, and sharing wealth
fairly were fundamental to his thinking. The early
revolutionaries were searching for an ideology to
guide them in their struggle to free the peasants
and working classes from what they saw as
exploitation by the landlords and the factory and
mill owners, in collusion with the ruling elite.

The Chinese Communist Party borrowed many
ideas from its Soviet counterpart, and it was not
really until 1949 that Mao Zedong's thought
developed independently. Mao constantly urged
the Chinese to identify with the peasants and with
the poorer members of
society, so the slogan "the
poorer the better" became
part of China's thinking in the
1950s, '60s, and '70s. People
shunned personal adornment,
such as jewelry, or pictures on
their walls, and if someone

had a new jacket or pair of trousers, they would
hide it under an old, torn one. The metaphor of the
"iron rice bowl" is also part of Maoist philosophy.
People were allocated a secure (but low-paid) job
for life and an iron rice bowl to eat from that could

never break, but the (metaphorical) bowl was only filled with a small quantity of low-quality rice.

At first the Communists followed their own philosophy—but this self-denial did not last. By the 1960s, sheltered behind high walls, the new Communist emperors were starting to partake of many of the pleasures of life that they did not allow anyone else to enjoy. The official Chinese verdict on Mao nowadays is that he was "70 percent good, 30 percent bad" and that the Cultural Revolution was "a mistake." Nevertheless, his portrait still hangs over the gateway to the Forbidden City, and his embalmed body (which may, according to popular rumor, have been replaced by a waxwork) still has a huge tomb all to itself in Tiananmen Square. Children still study some of his teachings in school, and his role in helping to rid China of the Japanese invaders and the Guomindang army of Chiang Kai Shek is undisputed. The slogan "The poorer the better," has long been replaced by Deng Xiao Ping's much more popular version, "To get rich is glorious"; yet it would still be considered discourteous for the visiting foreigner to criticize Mao, even though Chinese will often do so.

Many of these elements are reflected in Chinese attitudes today, especially now that the veneer of Communism seems to be wearing thin. Patience is a virtue inculcated into the Chinese from time immemorial, as they have had to put up with more tyranny, anarchy, and misrule than any Western people. It takes a lot to provoke a Chinese person to physical violence, though the crowded conditions mean that there are a lot of almost ritual shouting matches in the streets.

YIN AND YANG

For thousands of years, Chinese cosmology has seen the universe as being divided into two opposing yet complementary aspects, the primal forces or modes of creation of *yin* and *yang*. These terms will be well known to anyone familiar with the classic of divination, the *Yi Qing*, or *Book of Changes*. Although they represent polar opposites, as each force reaches its extreme it produces its opposite, creating a never-ending cycle, both on the physical and metaphysical planes. Yin corresponds to earth, moon, female, cold, and dark, whereas Yang corresponds to heaven, sun, male, heat, and brightness. The dragon was the embodiment of Yang, and the sun is still known in everyday speech as the Great Yang (*tai yang*). As Yin and Yang alternate, so night is followed by day, and the seasons rotate. The principles of Yin and Yang provided the foundation for divination, medicine, and cosmological theories. The pictorial representation of these polarities is a circle, containing a dark shape surrounding a bright nucleus, and its opposite. It is a way of showing that pure male and female do not exist: each contains its opposite. This principle of balancing forces is embedded in Chinese thought.

FENG SHUI

The practice of Feng Shui has become very fashionable in the West recently. In China its popularity is waning a little, except in the south and in Hong Kong. *Feng* is the Chinese word for wind; *shui* means water. This refers to the traditional Chinese belief that there are influences in the natural environment that affect people's fortunes. Every hill, field, and body of water is taken into account in matters such as the siting of graves, temples, homes, and, especially these days, offices. Since the calculations and esoteric knowledge needed for choosing an auspicious site are very complex, families or organizations will call in an expert geomancer, often at considerable expense, and consult him before any decisions are made.

Whereas in the West proposals to build new houses or offices on open ground may be objected to on environmental or historical grounds, in southern China villagers often protest against a new building because it would damage the existing Feng Shui of the area.

PRAGMATISM

The Chinese are pragmatists first and foremost, and their aim nowadays is pretty similar to that of families in other parts of the world: to give their children a good education, help them get a decent job, to improve their own level of culture and education, and to be able to relax a little and enjoy life. So long as the Chinese Communist Party provides them with the means to achieve these aims it is likely to stay in power: though some commentators believe that when a certain overall level of affluence has been reached, the Chinese may press for more and more freedom.

The young urban Chinese are very like their counterparts anywhere else in the world— hedonistic, with a lot of disposable income, hardworking, but also fun loving, and not too interested in China's bloodstained past. The peasants, too, have ambitions, and many have become rich.

China's new underclass are the millions of migrant workers who spend their lives trudging from one poorly paid, insecure, and often dangerous job to another, barely seeing their families from one year to the next. Nonetheless, the prosperity of the new China is being built with their efforts, and the Chinese government, recognizing that fact (and dreading the social unrest that could follow if millions of unemployed migrant workers became organized), is actively trying to help them with training schemes, resettlement packages, and so on, not dissimilar to Western governments' attempts to help the unemployed. Add to this the fact that many migrant workers still have some land and many come from farming families, so at least they have some means of subsistence. They also rarely have debts and frequently have some savings.

CITIZENS OF THE MIDDLE KINGDOM

The Chinese consciousness of their own identity is still strong, and they are rightly proud of their ancient culture and their rapid economic progress. But the old arrogance has gone, to be replaced by an excitement about the possibilities of the new world order. There is still a strong undercurrent of nationalism, however, that can turn rapidly against foreigners, bringing echoes of more troubled and hate-filled times.

Many people in the Asia-Pacific region have dwelt on the strange appearance of Europeans. The Chinese described them as ghostlike or hairy. Even ten years ago, the term *yang guize*, "foreign devils," was frequently overheard by visitors to China—although it could equally well be translated as "foreign ghost," which speaks as much of their pale skins and unusual amount of body hair as of their wickedness. In Hong Kong, expatriate Westerners living among the resident Chinese grew so used to being called *gweilos* (the Cantonese version of "foreign devils") that they themselves used the word affectionately to describe their community. As a foreigner in China, it is unlikely that you will ever be taken for a Chinese, and therefore allowances will be made for you. But it is still a good idea to watch what the Chinese people do in certain social and business situations, and to try to behave in a way compatible with this.

Broadly speaking, throughout Southeast Asia, Westerners are regarded as educated and wealthy, though scruffy ones are referred to by the derogatory term "hippies." They are thought to be punctual and honest, if somewhat aloof and unfriendly. Americans and Europeans are, however, not seen as being family oriented, and rumors circulate about the difficulties faced by older people in Western society. Westerners are also often assumed to have lax sexual morals.

Outside the main cities, in the remote rural areas, many people may never have actually seen a "real" foreigner before—though they will probably have spotted a few on TV, as many foreign films are shown nowadays. People of African origin are a particular object of curiosity, and as late as the 1990s African students at Tianjin University told how they had been approached in the streets by Chinese peasants, who rubbed at the skin on their arms and asked them why they did not wash. Other foreigners in remoter areas have found that, even when they try to speak Chinese, they are still not understood because the face that is making the sounds looks so strange!

In the cities nowadays foreigners will largely be ignored, as there are so many of them, but in remoter areas, or traveling on trains or planes, they will be treated with courtesy and as an object of fascination and delight. Most Chinese who meet a foreigner on his or her travels will tend to take a personal responsibility for the foreign guest's safety and happiness while in China.

ATTITUDES TO OVERSEAS CHINESE
The writer and celebrity Chinese chef Ken Hom has described the strange homesickness for

somewhere you have never been as a feeling familiar to the millions who are part of the Chinese diaspora. He writes: "You can go home again. The question is, what, or where is home? To a Chinese-American or any 'overseas Chinese,' emotional ambiguities are built into any answer. The Chinese experience outside of China has created what has been called 'sojourner mentality.' No matter what economic success emigrant Chinese achieve, the pull of the homeland remains powerful."

Yet if you are a visitor of Chinese origin, perhaps one who has grown up in the USA or Europe, expectations of you are likely to be high. You are expected to bring expensive gifts, sometimes for an entire extended family (a village-full is not unusual), and yet be suitably humbled by China's achievements—a slight contradiction. This can lead to problems and to resentment on both sides, as well as incredulity when it emerges that the overseas Chinese person cannot speak Mandarin.

On the other hand, the overseas Chinese visitor can blend into the crowd and pass unnoticed if he or she wants to. The only way a foreigner can do this is by buying a big straw hat to hide under.

PATIENCE IS A VIRTUE

In the PRC there can be a lot of red tape involved in what might seem the simplest of procedures—buying plane tickets, or changing money at a bank, for example—and it is essential to learn to accept such inconveniences gracefully. Impatience is seen by the Chinese as a serious character flaw. Trying to stick to a tight schedule in China is often not possible, though it is getting easier as more private travel agencies, banks, and other useful places appear on the scene to compete with the slow and sleepy state-run versions.

LOSING FACE

The Chinese are keen not to be seen to "lose face," or be shown up in a negative light in front of other people. If they cannot or do not want to answer a difficult question, the Chinese may laugh to cover their embarrassment. It could mean that the visitor has said something that has not been understood, or the Chinese person is unsure of his ground on some point. Equally, a foreigner loses face by becoming angry or upset. The phrase "It is not convenient" is often polite code for saying that something is impossible, or difficult, but that the Chinese person would rather not explain all the niceties of the situation at that moment. It is possible to push gently at a seemingly closed door, but do not try to kick it down. You can be a little insistent—but not too much. It is not at all rude to come back to a problem at a later stage, when there has been time for the Chinese person to discuss the issue privately with other people. He or she will take pride in raising the issue again themselves when it has been sorted out.

MEN AND WOMEN

If you are dealing with someone of the opposite sex, there is unlikely to be any touching after the initial handshake, but members of the same sex do tend to touch each other more than in the West, and women frequently emphasize a point by patting each other on the arm. In some places away from large urban centers, you may well see young people of the same sex walking along the street hand in hand. In Chinese society this is no more than an expression of friendship, just as it used to be in the Catholic countries of southern Europe. There are, of course, gay men and women in China, but the topic is still pretty much taboo and homosexuals have to be discreet.Openly "camp" behavior or dressing outrageously is still likely to draw too much unwelcome attention outside the major cities such as Shanghai or Beijing.

ATTITUDES TO WOMEN

One of the Communists' painfully slow but ultimately successful campaigns has been to give women in Chinese society equal rank with men. There is still a traditional preference for sons over daughters among the peasantry, which led to the killing of baby girls (an ancient "feudal" practice condemned by the government but which has proved hard to stamp out). As recently as 1949, when the Communists took power, the barbaric tradition of binding women's feet to keep them from growing "big and ugly" was still in force, despite earlier efforts to ban it in 1912. Another genuine "great leap forward" for women in the PRC has been the availability of contraception and childcare. Mao's statement that "women hold up half the sky" is coming true at last as a whole generation of young, clever, educated women take their place in the world of commerce, science, medicine, and the media. Progress for women seems to be slower in the rarefied atmosphere of Chinese politics. But foreign women traveling in China will not have any more problems than they would back home, and women working there will be accepted on equal terms.

THE MYTH OF CHINESE INSCRUTABILITY

In accounts of traditional China, Western writers often used to make the point that Chinese people were not given to being direct in conversation, and favored an oblique approach to almost all subjects; in fact you will probably find that the Chinese people you meet, while treating you very courteously, are often much more direct than many Westerners. Once they know you and trust you (which does not take long) they are as ready to show emotions as any other people. You can expect to be asked direct questions about your age, family, marital status, health, housing, car, and salary—and you, in turn, can ask them about the same sorts of things. Remember to be a little cautious (and sensitive) when talking about the number of children someone has. The government's One Child policy has caused an enormous amount of anguish, and is best touched on lightly unless the person you are talking to appears to want to pursue the subject.

Many Westerners who have spent any time in China have made warm and long-lasting friendships with Chinese people. The differences in the cultures are intriguing and worth knowing about, for both sides, but they are not a barrier.

THE FAMILY

In many rich Western countries, the traditional family (two married parents, two children) is constantly said to be "in crisis." In China it is still regarded as the basis of society and of the individual's guarantee of happiness and security. Rigid rules about premarital sex and living together before marriage are relaxing a little, but unmarried mothers are still rare, divorce rates are low (though rising), and looking after elderly family members at home rather than exiling them to an old people's "home" is almost universal. In southern China especially, the family is often part of a much larger clan, whose duty is to help each other. Frequently, university fees or other large expenses are paid for by distant relations— especially if they live in Taiwan or the USA. Children are expected to show respect to their parents; this is the fundamental concept of *filial piety,* first defined by Confucius. "Filial piety is the basis of all virtue. It begins with one's parents, is kept up by serving one's sovereign, and ends up by establishing oneself [in life]."

Ironically, the One Child policy, limiting families to one child only, has had a negative effect on filial piety; the Chinese press regularly laments that it has created a generation of children who are worshiped by their adoring parents, and who, because they have no siblings, have not had to learn the tedious early lessons of sharing and compromising. The Chinese have dubbed these spoilt children "little emperors" and they can be seen everywhere in the richer towns, indulging in their favorite sport of "pester power," that is, getting their parents to buy them things. In the rural areas where many families have ignored the One Child policy, family life is less focused on the needs of one small person, more on the need of the whole household to pull together to create wealth (or just to survive).

The Chinese language has a whole range of titles for family members—auntie (*taitai*), small brother (*didi*), big brother (*gege*), and so on. Although the extended family is shrinking in the towns, these lovely old words will survive because many of them are also used for other people outside the immediate family—rather as in the West, before it was considered polite for children to call adults by their first name, children were told to call family friends "aunt" and "uncle."

BABIES AND CHILDREN

The Chinese love their own babies and children, and Westerners traveling with their children will find them the center of attention and compliments. It can be a bit overwhelming for very young Western children, unused to so much attention at home, who find their cheeks and legs pinched, and their arms patted and stroked almost beyond endurance, and who may have to pose for endless photos with their hordes of fans (curly blond or red hair especially can attract huge crowds in minutes). The Chinese love of children comes partly from the belief in the need for family and clan continuity, but also it springs from sheer joy in their freshness and enthusiasm in a country where life can still be quite dull, hard, and gray for many.

However a new phenomenon has emerged in recent years that has spoilt the innocent, shared enjoyment of children that used to make travel in China a pleasure for families. There has been a rise in kidnappings of small children; not of Westerners, who would be too prominent, but of Chinese children, whether it is babies who can be sold to childless parents or older children who have been taken to work as forced labor in factories and, almost unbelievably, in coal mines. Though not common, these terrible incidents have happened often enough to make Chinese parents who used never to worry about their children's safety in public very wary of leaving them alone. As a result of this, and of course of increased levels of petty crime as has happened everywhere in the world, the visitor will notice more and more "gated communities" in big towns—that is, apartment blocks that are fenced off and can only be entered through a gate which is guarded. These were almost unknown until recently, except for the political elite and for foreign residents.

RESPECT FOR OLD AGE AND ANCESTORS

Filial piety means that respect is paid to older people, and by extension to the ancestors. Westerners have heard vaguely of "ancestor worship"; a better way to describe it would be respect for one's ancestors. The only down-side of this tradition of venerating old age is that, until recently, anyone who held a position of power was more or less guaranteed to keep the job till he (it was usually a "he") died in office or retired grudgingly at about eighty years old. This did not do much for the country's economy or the chances of promotion of younger people with fresh new ideas. But as the free-market economy takes over, older people are happy enough to retire earlier and enjoy life. Many workers in their fifties have been made redundant and have had to retrain, but at least they do not suffer the same stigma as anyone over forty tends to in the youth-obsessed West.

The traditional festival of Qing Ming, when families bring offerings to the tombs of their ancestors, is still important today (see page 89).

EDUCATION

The Chinese have always valued learning and respected scholars. One of the worst effects of the Cultural Revolution was that a whole generation lost out on schooling. Nowadays, people are even more passionate about education as they move toward a modern, knowledge-based economy. Chinese school children and university students have enormous amounts of homework, and have to sit for very tough and competitive exams. Teachers and professors are highly respected (though not highly paid). Demand for a good education outstrips supply, and the government has encouraged the growth of fee-paying schools at all levels to help plug the gap. Online education and distance education on the TV and radio are also provided—ideal for such a huge country. Underfunding is a problem, and the government has pledged more money. But parents are increasingly expected to help out and many state schools are now charging fees. In poorer regions, access to secondary (and even primary) schooling is restricted; the World Bank

is working with the Chinese government to improve this situation.

Travelers to China who are interested in this aspect of life should read a short and very moving book called *Ma Yan—the Struggles and Hopes of a Chinese Schoolgirl.* It is the true story of thirteen-year-old Ma and her family. They live in Ningxia, one of the poorest regions in China and Ma Yan's diary, documenting her longing to go to school and the dire poverty of her community, was given to a passing French journalist. It became a best seller in France and has been translated into seventeen languages.

GUANGXI, OR SOCIAL NETWORKING CHINESE STYLE

Networking, or using *guangxi,* was for centuries the main way of getting anything done—finding a marriage partner, a school or job for your child, a market for your product, a place to live, or a trip overseas. Favors were given and returned in an unspoken web of complex relationships. The "trusted networks" of the Chinese are based on two or more persons sharing a commonality of identification. On the whole, it is kinship and family ties that form the basis of Chinese *guangxi* because of the moral obligation of relatives to help each other. But nonrelatives and foreigners can be incorporated into the network. Marital, family, and friendship bonds are important in *guangxi*: so are other ties such as exchanges of vows of blood brotherhood. *Guangxi* ties can also be established by appealing to the real or imaginary ties between people bearing the same Chinese surnames. This does not presuppose common ancestry, though early migrants to Southeast Asia often banded together in surname associations to provide mutual assistance.

Friendship ties developed through coresidence, schooling, and other shared social experiences can also form the basis of *guangxi*. The overseas Chinese have long appreciated the value of kinship and locality links in business, in minimizing risks, transaction costs, and the uncertainties of external economic relationships. Their trading networks span Southeast Asia, and can be very helpful to entrepreneurs wishing to set up joint ventures, or to locate new suppliers in mainland China. Many Chinese firms engage non-Chinese partners, but, compared with their traditional bonds, these purely functional ties are less strong.

chapter three

THE CHINESE AT HOME

LIFESTYLES AND HOUSING

In today's more relaxed political climate, it is becoming increasingly common for the Chinese to invite their foreign friends home for dinner, and even to stay in their homes, something that would have been unthinkable a few years ago. The visit can be carried out quite openly. No Party vigilante will be hovering at the entrance to the apartment building inquiring whom you are visiting or why—though curious neighbors may well take this role on for themselves! The Chinese are used to living cheek by jowl, and take a lot of interest in each other's comings and goings. You should be prepared to be the center of attention. Chinese inviting Westerners to their home often invite relatives, neighbors, and friends to drop in to inspect the visitor—especially if some of them speak English or the native tongue of the guest. This is a chance for lighthearted conversation, rather than serious discussion of topical issues.

The Chinese are extremely hospitable. Tea will be served the moment the guest walks through the door, usually accompanied by various snacks, such as rice crackers, roasted watermelon or sunflower seeds, peanuts, or preserved or fresh fruit. One can nibble at one or two of these offerings, but there is no obligation to keep snacking—especially as there is likely to be a substantial meal served at a later stage.

Unlike the Japanese, who generally entertain in public places due to embarrassment at the cramped conditions at home, the Chinese seem to be quite happy to throw open their homes to visitors, no matter how humble the dwelling.

With the rapid demolition of many of the traditional courtyard homes that made cities like Beijing so attractive in the past, most ordinary Chinese now live in high-rise apartment blocks. These tend to be very basic, and even new ones often have a raw, unfinished look. The individual home is likely to be somewhat small and cramped by Western standards. There may be a bed in the

living room, which provides valuable additional seating when visitors come. Dinner may be served on a small table crammed into a corner between the front door and the toilet. Nevertheless, from the host's point of view, this is likely to be a considerable improvement on the family's previous accommodation. The PRC has severe housing problems, which it is trying to overcome, so for most people in this overcrowded country the fact of having a roof over their head, a toilet and kitchen that are not shared with other families, and hot and cold running water, is sufficient blessing.

The per capita living space in most major cities is only 76.4 square feet (7.1 sq. m). People live on top of each other with little privacy. Conflicts are common over minor issues—a playful child, a noisy radio. A goal of most Chinese is to move into new and larger houses, but prices are high and most will have to wait years for their dream home. But the Chinese can now buy their own homes, and many rich urban couples are doing that; peasant families tend to own their homes, and whenever they have some spare cash they add another room or another floor. (Unlike Westerners, they do not need to worry too much about planning permission.)

As more young people get married, start families, and begin to enjoy more freedom to move around the country, the traditional extended family is starting to break up. In the main cities, three or even four generations living under one roof is becoming less common with each passing year.

Although the exterior may not look attractive, the Chinese do their best to make the interior of their own homes as pleasing and comfortable as their limited budgets allow. The homes the Westerner is likely to visit will be fairly well furnished. With growing affluence, the gap between them and the average Western home is narrowing. Invariably, there will be a color TV, a DVD or CD player, telephone, and, increasingly, a computer. Many Western visitors have realized that their TV and computer back home are more old-fashioned than the ones their Chinese hosts possess. Many high-tech Japanese goods are now manufactured in China, so the Chinese market seems to get its pick of newer models several years before Western Europe does! In the kitchen there will be a refrigerator, a washing machine, and a microwave oven—these, too, are made in China. Manufacturers of dishwashers are optimistic that this will be the next acquisition for urban families. Because of limited space, the home will tend to look rather overcrowded, with every inch of space used for storage. There are rarely carpets on the floors, as the floors are swept clean rather than vacuumed. Many families remove their shoes when inside their homes—take your cue from your hosts.

Entertainment normally takes place at the weekend, especially now that the move to a five-day working week has given urban residents more free time. Both husband and wife normally work, and with the need to do shopping on the way home, the day away from home can be a long one. In addition, even young primary schoolchildren have a lot of homework, and the arrival of a foreign visitor during the working week would not be conducive to study.

Home entertainment centers on the television. Apart from regular TV programs, many Chinese families enjoy watching Video Compact Disc (VCD) or DVD versions of popular foreign movies. These will almost invariably be pirate versions bought on the streets at  very low cost—something the government is trying to stamp out, but with limited success so far.

SOCIAL RELATIONS AND OCCUPATIONS

On the whole, the visitor to China will tend to mix socially with the urban, middle-class Chinese who have a wide knowledge of international affairs and a love of culture. These people often have more in common with the average Westerner than with the poorer, rural inhabitants of their own country.

Although the Western visitor may meet other people on his travels, conversation will be rather limited; first, because of this huge gulf in knowledge of the wider world between the poorer peasants and the more educated classes; and second, because of the language barrier— even if you learn enough Chinese to carry on a simple conversation, the regional accents and dialects outside the big cities can be pretty impenetrable even for the Chinese themselves.

The types of jobs done by people in China are not dissimilar from those in the West—teachers, doctors, journalists, businessmen, and so on. There are, mercifully, fewer Chinese whose lives are blighted by being stuck in a stifling government bureaucracy nowadays, although, compared with many Western countries, there are still a lot of people who earn their living as minor government officials. But at least the trend is for jobs to be awarded on merit and advertised openly in the newspapers, rather than dished out to graduates by the universities, or as a result of good *guangxi*. This means people are not only much busier at work than they used to be, but also have greater job satisfaction and higher salaries. There is greater job security than in the West, and some big state-run "work units," or *danwei*, still provide everything for their employees and their families, from housing to schools to hospital care. This pattern of cradle-to-grave social provision centered on the work unit is fragmenting rapidly though.

PRESENTS

When Chinese visitors come to the West they invariably bring a number of small, typically Chinese presents for their hosts, and this is a good custom to imitate. For home visits as a friend, or for business trips, small decorative items such as paperweights or china are acceptable. Whiskey (the better brands) and foreign cigarettes go over well, but the Chinese do not have as sweet a tooth as Westerners, so do not buy chocolates. It used to be well nigh impossible to find fresh flowers or plants in the shops in China, but there are florists springing up everywhere now and bringing an indoor house plant to your hosts in a nice flower pot is very welcome, as their apartments can be rather drab by Western standards. The florists will take enormous care over wrapping and preparing the plant to give, and prices are absurdly cheap. Little gifts of food, such as more expensive fresh fruit, are also welcome, and again, easy to buy nowadays.

Your interpreter would probably appreciate an English book or a good recording of a book or play. CDs of good classical, jazz, or pop music are popular too, as China's CD piracy industry is not very selective and many of the pirated CDs are of abysmal quality.

For business travelers the ettiquette is a bit different. The most senior of the people you will be dealing with will expect a bigger present, though if it is at all sizeable it might be a good idea to make it plain that you are giving it to him or her for the whole group. Otherwise, suitable gifts could be company pens (with refills, if needed), or company ties, ashtrays, or small pieces of glass.

It has become harder to find suitable gifts for Chinese people as so many items that we buy in the West, at a mark-up of several hundred percent, are now manufactured in China. But it is the thought that counts, rather than the gift itself.

One custom that can upset the unwary visitor is that if the present is wrapped, many Chinese people will not unwrap it while their visitor is there, but will stow it away hurriedly on top of a cupboard out of sight. This does not mean they are displeased with it; it is simply "not done" to open the gift in front of the donor.

Remember This
One gift to avoid is a clock or a watch. The Chinese words for "to give a clock" sound exactly the same as the words for "to take someone to their death."

CHINESE NAMES
In China the surname precedes the personal name, since the family group or clan has traditionally been seen as more important than the individual.

Zhang Hua is thus Mr. Zhang, not Mr. Hua. Sometimes, though, the Chinese adopt the Western practice of putting the personal name before their surname. So it is a good idea, especially when confronted with a Chinese name of only two syllables, such as Jing Wang, to check whether the bearer of that name is a Mr./Ms. Jing, or a Mr./Ms.Wang.

In addressing the Chinese people you meet it is best to use Mr., Mrs., Miss, plus their surnames: Chinese people are more formal than many Westerners. The favored all-purpose title used by the Communists, *tongjia* or "Comrade," has dropped out of use in recent years. If you use it now you may find that it makes people laugh. Many older titles have come back into fashion, the Chinese equivalents of Sir/Madam/Miss.

You may also find that the Chinese refer to one another by their job-title—Mayor Wang, Manager Li, Teacher Zhang, and so on. This is a direct translation of the way they would normally refer to one another in Chinese, and is a useful habit to adopt, because you are almost bound to meet several people who share the same surname, and it will help you keep them separate in your mind.

An affectionate nickname for the Chinese peasant is "*lao bai xing,*" or "Old Hundred Names." There are in fact four-hundred-and-thirty-eight Chinese surnames, but that is still a tiny number considering the size of the Chinese population. Only thirty names have two syllables; the rest are of one syllable only, and some of the commonest are Zhang, Wang,

Wu, Zhao, and Li. Personal names can be of either one or two syllables and are very often chosen according to a prearranged plan, sometimes one that the family has adhered to for generations. The children of each generation—and this includes those cousins who are children of one's father's brothers—may all have a "generation" character in common: Li Weiguang, for instance, may have a younger brother or cousin called Li Weiguo, and a sister called Li Weiling, where Li is the family's surname and Wei the "generation" character.

The sound and the meanings of names are very important in China. If you can find a kind person to think up a good Chinese name for you, that fits your Western name phonetically and also carries an attractive and positive meaning, then when you hand over your business card, it will have much more impact on the people you meet. When Chinese people choose Western names the choice is equally important, and if you are going to work with Chinese colleagues and help them choose English names for themselves, take a name dictionary.

Names Matter

One English person fell foul of this when training staff to work in a new luxury hotel in Guangzhou. She chose the name George for one young trainee—but when she told him the story of St. George killing the dragon in Roman times (central to Western folklore) he was horrified, as he had been born in the Year of the Dragon. A replacement name was swiftly chosen.

It is not considered respectful for children to use their father's personal name, and in more old-fashioned families the wife does not do so either. If a foreign visitor of the opposite sex uses the wife's or husband's personal name this can be quite embarrassing. So if you have a friend called Professor Zhang Dai Lin, call him or her (many names can belong to either a man or a woman in China) Professor Zhang, *not* Dai Lin, or at least not until you know him or her very well indeed.

A more informal way of addressing people is by using their surname and the word *xiao* or *lao* in front of it. *Xiao* means "little" or "young"; *lao* means "old." The cutoff point is around thirty-five; so if you are a foreigner who starts visiting China when you are still *Xiao* Smith, one day you will have to get used to being called *Lao* Smith. Just remember that the Chinese are showing respect for your advancing age, even though you might rather have hoped that no one would notice it. When someone is really old the word *lao* is still used—but its position changes. China's late president Deng Xiao Ping lived well into his nineties and was known respectfully as "Deng Lao." Using *xiao* and *lao* is completely acceptable among friends and colleagues, and foreigners find it a welcome way to handle the intricacies of Chinese names. But *don't* use it the first time you meet; wait until you know someone well, and then you can ask if they mind. As for your own name, in business dealings it is best initially to call yourself Mr. Smith, Miss Jones, or Mrs. Evans; keep the use of your first name for friends.

Separate Identities

A custom that seems specially designed to fool the foreigner is that most Chinese women do not change their surnames when they marry. It is possible to know Mrs. Hu and Mr. Li for a long time without realizing that they are actually married to each other.

OVERCOMING THE LANGUAGE BARRIER

Because of upheavals in the education system during the Cultural Revolution and afterward, the amount of English that your Chinese friends and contacts know will vary considerably. English is now taught at all levels of the school system, and the thirst for learning it is growing by the day. But even those who do know some English will have had less practice in speaking it than in reading or writing. Some Chinese speak exceptionally good English; other, older, Chinese may know none at all, having had to learn Russian or Japanese at school or not had any schooling at all.

Be patient when speaking, use short sentences, speak a little more slowly than usual if you suspect you are not being understood, and try not to use unnecessarily difficult words, or slang. Be prepared to rephrase what you have just said, rather than just repeat it, and be sure not to raise your voice. In Taiwan, many Chinese people are more attuned to American pronunciation than to British. If you are using an interpreter, try not to say too much at a time—give her (or him) a chance to interpret a manageable amount before you move on to the next sentence. It is important to maintain eye contact with the person you are talking to (though not all the time, of course), rather than solely with the interpreter. If you can learn some simple Chinese phrases (more about this in Chapter 10) you will find it rewarding.

MEETING AND GREETING
Shake Hands
On meeting someone, of either sex and any age apart from very young children, the usual practice

is to shake hands, often for a much longer time than would be usual in the West. This may be accompanied by a respectful nod. If you are being introduced to a group of people, make sure to shake hands with all of them. From then on, as far as physical contact is concerned, take your cue from the person you are talking to.

Stand Up

In the ever-more-informal West, the custom of standing up when someone to whom you have not yet been introduced comes into the room has almost vanished. In China it would be rude not to stand up and shake hands with the new person, and to wait until they have asked you to sit down before you collapse back into your armchair. When in doubt in China, err on the side of formality. The only exception is if you are in a formal meeting at a workplace and someone very junior tiptoes in shyly to whisper to a colleague, usually about arrangements for food or transport. Just smile politely; do not leap up and start shaking hands. When presenting a name card, hold it with both hands and take any which you receive with both hands too, inclining your head forward as you do so.

BODY LANGUAGE

Compared with some of the more deeply religious and therefore elaborately ritualized societies in

Asia, such as India, Indonesia, or Japan, behavior in China is simple and straightforward. Years of identifying with the "worker, peasant, soldier" (that is, the poorest and least educated ranks of society) have made the Chinese relatively informal and relaxed. One thing you are unlikely to see (and which you should certainly not do) is kissing in public; hugging and other exuberant "touchy-feely" Western body language is rare.

Until recently it was *de rigueur* to belch loudly after a meal to show your appreciation: this, too, was part of identifying with the masses in terms of social behavior. The Chinese who have had contact with Westerners have noticed that this does not go over well with their guests, and have abandoned the practice.

Among the poorer people, spitting and very loud throat clearing, caused in the north by the dust from the Gobi Desert, and all over China by far too much smoking, is a widespread and unpleasant habit that you just have to learn to put up with. There have been numerous public health campaigns against it, with limited success. Nevertheless, if *you* have a cold and need to blow your nose, try to go outside the room—it is considered disgusting by many Chinese to do this in front of other people.

You should also make sure that you cover up bare feet in the summer (socks worn with sandals may be uncool in the West but they are a must in China), and dress modestly and conventionally.

EXITS AND ENTRANCES

Whether you are joining a new friend for a meal, going to an old friend's house, or taking part in a business meeting, punctuality is vital. The Chinese consider it very rude to be late, even by a few minutes. Of course, if you are unavoidably delayed (traffic jams have become a major problem in China's big cities), you should phone ahead and apologize, as everyone now has access to a telephone and often one or more cell phones as well.

Chinese people rise early and go to bed early, so lunch will probably be at noon, or even before, and evening banquets are likely to begin at six. Meals, meetings, and visits will end promptly. Once the meal is over (and it could last for a long time), the visitors may chat for a few minutes but should then get up and go. There is none of the prolonged after-dinner coffee drinking so common in the West, and departure soon after the end of the meal is the rule in China. It is polite for your hosts to come all the way to the main door, or to see you into your taxi, to say good-bye. If you are the host, you should do the same.

BOY MEETS GIRL

It is only recently that young Chinese men and women have stopped having to ask the permission of their superiors in their *danweis* (work units) to get engaged or married. This was in part an attempt to stop the forced early marriages of old China, and the minimum age for getting married (or even dating) was set at around twenty-five. Things are freer and easier now, though it is still hard for young couples to find somewhere private to go, and almost unheard of to live together before marriage (partly because of the shortage of accommodation). If a Chinese girl and boy start dating, it is usually assumed that they will get married eventually. It is important for visiting Westerners to be aware of this—what they may see as a casual affair is likely to be taken much more seriously by the Chinese partner who may expect and hope that what is for them a "serious" love affair will lead to marriage. Coupled with the fact that the attraction of life in the West is still very strong, it is easy for foreigners unwittingly to abuse their power. That said, there are plenty of other entertainments available in the nightclubs and bars these days for lonely visitors, men or women.

HOBBIES

More leisure, freedom, and money have given many Chinese the chance to take up hobbies. These are fairly low-key as the Chinese are very careful with their money, but eating out, playing and watching sports, doing *taijiquan* (a meditative exercise, see also *qigong*, page 103), stamp collecting, keeping pet birds, reading, playing mah-jong and chess, ballroom dancing and going to discos and karaoke bars, watching TV, going to the cinema and theater, and surfing the Internet are all enjoyed in the cities (there are far fewer facilities in the rural areas). Increasingly, shopping in the growing number of bustling, modern department stores is done for pleasure rather than just to gather the bare necessities of life. The next big boom will be when the Chinese become rich enough for travel abroad to become a reality for the many, rather than just the favored few.

chapter four

RELIGION, FESTIVALS, & RITUALS

MANY RELIGIONS AND NONE

Official policy is to tolerate but not to encourage religion. The Constitution provides for freedom of religious belief and forbids discrimination against believers and nonbelievers, though theory and practice do not always match. There are many different religions in China: about 100 million people are Buddhists; an estimated 18 million are Muslims; 10 million are Protestants, and 4 million Catholics. These are simply estimates though, as many people in China keep their religion very private.

Although the majority of Chinese are secular and atheist, traditional festivals and the beliefs and rituals attached to them are important in that they give a structure to the year, and help to define the meaning of life and of people's position in the world at large and within their families. One Chinese author writes: "The Chinese are more concerned with propitiating devils than with worshiping gods," and many ceremonies do just that. Legendary Chinese gods—such as the semidivine Monkey, who accompanied the monk Hsuanchuong on a pilgrimage, as related in the epic *Journey to the Western Paradise*—seem to Western eyes to be selfish, cruel, and capricious.

TRADITIONAL FESTIVALS AND NATIONAL HOLIDAYS

There were many festivals in the traditional Chinese lunar calendar, and several of these are still celebrated throughout the Chinese world. The first and most important is known in the West as Chinese New Year and in the PRC as the Spring Festival (so called because in the PRC January 1 is officially New Year).

Chinese New Year

This has always been the time for family reunions. It falls around the middle of February, during the slack period of the farming year—in the PRC more than three-quarters of the population work in agriculture—which means that almost everyone can take a few days' holiday.

The atmosphere is very festive—people dress in new clothes, and strings of very noisy firecrackers are set off at all hours of the day and night. The tradition is that this will scare away any evil spirits lurking about, and also welcome in the New Year. But recently the use of firecrackers has been restricted in the cities. There is also a lot of feasting.

Families will make, and eat, hundreds of *jiaozi* (stuffed dumplings that are supposed to be shaped like gold ingots and therefore bring good luck), and they will eat much more meat than usual, and perhaps a special sticky New Year cake called *niangao*. Younger members of the family should pay their respects to the older members (and, in more traditional homes, to the ancestors as well), and the children will be given small red envelopes of money. A lot of visiting goes on between relatives and friends, and houses are decorated with special New Year pictures and matching couplets written on red paper. (Red is the lucky color in China.) In many places, this will also be the occasion to watch a Lion Dance, and for all-night gambling sessions. It is also a time for payment of debts.

Each year is named after a particular animal from the Chinese horoscope. There are twelve animals altogether, and a Chinese person will always be able to tell you which animal he "belongs" to—that is, which animal is associated with the year in which he was born. The order in which the twelve-year cycle repeats itself is: Rat, Ox, Tiger, Hare, Dragon, Snake, Horse, Sheep (or Goat), Monkey, Cockerel, Dog, and Pig. In this system, 2007 was the year of the Pig, 2008 was the year of the Rat, and so on. Just as the different star signs in the Western horoscope, such as Virgo, Pisces, Taurus, and so on, have certain characteristics associated with them, so do the Chinese animals.

Qing Ming Festival

On the festival of Qing Ming, which takes place on the third day of the third month in the spring, families visit the tombs of their ancestors, clean them, and make offerings of cooked meats, fish, fruit, and wine. They then picnic on the food themselves, sitting near the tombs. Many families used to have their own ancestral halls where the wooden tablets with names of their male ancestors were kept. (Thousands of these places were smashed to pieces by the Red Guards in the 1960s.) From the tablets, families could be traced back several hundred years or more. In the town of Qufu, where Confucius was born, almost the whole town seems to have the same surname as his—Kong—and can therefore trace their families back to about 500 BCE.

Dragon Boat Festival

The Dragon Boat Festival (*Duan Yang Jie*, or *Duan Wu Jie*) falls on the fifth day of the fifth lunar month. It is a very ancient festival whose origins have been lost in the mists of time, but these days it is associated with Qu Yuan, a loyal minister of Chu (an ancient state in the south of China), who committed suicide in the third century BCE by jumping into a local river when the King of Chu refused to listen to his good advice. There are lively races between long, thin "dragon boats" to the rhythm of drums, and these are said by some people to represent attempts to rescue Qu Yuan. Special packets of glutinous rice (*zongzi*) wrapped in leaves are eaten, and these are said to have been intended for the fish (or, in some versions, the dragon) in the river, so that they would eat them and leave Qu Yuan alone. It is easier to see this festival in the south of China, and in Hong Kong, where, as has been noted, people keep more to the old traditions. There is also a distinct lack of suitable rivers for boat racing in the arid north!

The Mid-Fall Festival

The Mid-Fall Festival, or the Moon Festival, occurs on the fifteenth day of the eighth lunar month (around mid-September), at a time when the moon is supposed to be brighter and fuller than at any other time of the year. It is an equivalent of the West's Harvest Festival, celebrated by some Christians, and is traditionally held in honor of the moon goddess, Chang-O. Another useful resident of the moon, Yue Lao, a matchmaker, has his work cut out at this time of year, tying couples together with invisible red silk thread.

Like the Spring Festival, this, too, is a festival when the family gets together, sitting around a circular table to symbolize continuity, possibly to sing folk songs (or, these days, karaoke), or to display fancy lanterns, but mostly to admire the moon and eat "moon-cakes." These are round cakes stuffed with a variety of things such as lotus-seed paste, fruit, nuts, ham, or egg yolk.

The fillings vary according to the different areas of China. Yet another legend that has become intertwined with the Moon Festival is that Chinese rebels who wanted to overthrow the Mongols during the Yuan dynasty sent messages to each other hidden inside moon cakes. Most foreigners do not find moon cakes sweet enough, but they look beautiful and make good presents.

Official PRC Festivals

As well as Labor Day on May 1, there is Chinese Youth Day on May 4, Army Day on August 1, and National Day on October 1. There is nothing much of interest for the visitor to see on these days. The traditional Soviet-style parades of tanks and heavy guns along the main streets of Beijing have been quietly dropped; instead people get quite a lot of time off work (something new and much appreciated) and are encouraged to go out and spend money in the shops, apparently with great success judging by the crowds. In 2009, as the economic crisis started to bite, a Chinese magazine called *Liaowang* (*Outlook*) wrote that "To consume is to love one's country. Patriotism doesn't just

NATIONAL HOLIDAYS (SOLAR CALENDAR)	
New Year	January 1
Spring Festival (Lunar New Year)	February 11-14 (three days)
International Working Women's Day	March 8
Labor Day	May 1
Chinese Youth Day	May 4
International Children's Day	June 1
Army Day	August 1
Teachers' Day	September 10
National Day	October 1 (two days)

TRADITIONAL FESTIVALS (LUNAR CALENDAR)	
Chun Jie, Chinese New Year/ Spring Festival	Coincides with the new moon in late January/early February
Yuan Xiao Jie, Lantern Festival	First full moon after Spring Festival
Qing Ming Jie, Pure Brightness Day	Third day of the third month in Spring
Duan Wu Jie, Dragon Boat Festival	Fifth day of fifth lunar month
Zhong Qiu Jie, Mid-Fall Festival	Fifteenth day of the eighth lunar month

mean shedding one's blood on the battlefield, but in these times when our economy is afflicted by the global crisis, going out and consuming is real patriotism."

Avoid going to China on National Day or around the Chinese New Year if you have work to do, as, rather like Christmas in the West, you will have trouble finding anyone in their offices. Christmas Day itself is an ordinary working day in China—but Christmas, Chinese style, has been adopted in the big cities, with Santa Claus and shopping as its main rationale.

BIRTHDAYS, WEDDINGS, AND FUNERALS
Births

The birth of a child, particularly a son, is regarded as a very lucky event; continuity of the family is assured and there will be a feast held a month after the child's birth, in which hard-boiled eggs with the shells dyed red are eaten. There are some traditional Chinese practices concerning the care of the mother and baby after the birth: the mother does not wash her hair for a month as this is thought to weaken her, and the baby is often bound tightly in a white cloth, reminiscent of the infant Jesus being "wrapped in swaddling bands"; this was originally thought to keep the baby's legs straight after birth, though of course if the child's legs did end up bent, this would have been caused by malnutrition. Birthdays as such are not usually celebrated in China. By the traditional calendar, age is reckoned from the moment of conception, not birth, so a child is already considered to be one year old on the day it is born. There is a birthday for everyone, which falls on the seventh day of the Chinese New Year.

Weddings

Weddings in China have always been colorful and expensive occasions; today at least most modern brides and grooms get to choose their own partners. In the past, it was the family who chose for them, and the bride and groom would only see each other on the day of the wedding.

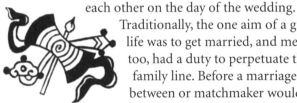 Traditionally, the one aim of a girl's life was to get married, and men, too, had a duty to perpetuate the family line. Before a marriage, a go-between or matchmaker would be employed to sort out the details of what was basically a financial transaction. When all had been agreed, the bride (who was often no more than fourteen years old) would be conveyed from her parents' home though the streets in a sedan chair to the house of her new husband. No one would see her—the sedan chair was completely sealed, and there are even stories of brides being found dead from suffocation on arrival (which did not stop the "marriage" from taking place).

Another tradition, which the Communists put an end to, was that of the man taking concubines, either to give him more children, or simply because he grew bored with his first wife. Reports from

Shanghai and other big cities say concubines are back in vogue, as men and even some women now have more money and time for a varied sex life. But these modern-day concubines are not held prisoner as they would once have been, so it is an arrangement that seems to work for everyone. In Tibet polyandry was common, where one wife had several husbands, usually brothers or cousins. This is dying out now too.

A happy marriage was rare in old China, partly because the husband's mother was often cruel to the new bride. Widows did not remarry, as it was thought immoral to marry more than once. It is not surprising that from ancient times there have been secret societies of women who worshipped the goddess Kwan Yin and vowed never to marry. Many attached themselves for life to rich families as maids, and stayed there safely out of the reach of their parents and any would-be matchmakers.

Marriage in China now is viewed as being for life, fidelity is taken for granted, and divorce is possible but still rare. Husbands and wives both work and tend to share all the household tasks and

childcare. People feel sorry for someone who is not married, but there is no longer the same social pressure to marry. Weddings in town are celebrated in restaurants amid a great deal of noise, and the traditional color for anything to do with weddings is red.

Funerals

The many beliefs surrounding death in China have survived into the twenty-first century virtually intact, despite the endless political campaigns of the twentieth. Until recent times it was still the custom to bury clothing and jewels with the body. In Hong Kong, entire shops are devoted to selling paper money, paper furniture, cars, houses, and paper clothes that are burned and placed with the body on burial; even the non-religious will often pay a Buddhist or Daoist priest to say prayers (several hours long) and perform ceremonies for the soul of the dead person. Another custom that would be thought very strange in the West was that of buying the coffin in advance and storing it in the house. The Chinese, in other words, do not need to come to terms with their own mortality; they accept it as one of the most important events in the life cycle.

White is the color worn at funerals. If the deceased has made it to seventy—interestingly, the same age that is given in the Bible as the natural life span of Man—the death is not thought to be an occasion for serious grief, though there will be a lot of noisy ritual lamentation during the funeral procession.

The Chinese believe that the body needs to go into the next world intact, and so cremation is very unpopular. This presents a problem in the overcrowded cities where there simply is not enough space for graveyards. Another problem arising from the strongly held belief in the need for an intact corpse is that organ donation is rare in Chinese communities, though this affects overseas Chinese more; not many PRC hospitals are geared up yet for this sort of medicine.

chapter five

HEALTH & WELL-BEING

STAYING HEALTHY IN CHINA

If you fall ill in China, you should be able to arrange a visit to the doctor through the staff at your hotel. In the PRC this might entail a trip to the local hospital, but this is only because there is no such person as a general practitioner in China. It is very worrying for the Chinese, who see themselves as your hosts for as long as you are in their country, to have a sick foreigner on their hands, and they will make every effort to see that you are well cared for.

With normal precautions, such as avoiding unboiled water and dubious food sold by street vendors, most of China should not present too many health hazards. In the summer, inoculations against endemic Japanese encephalitis might be a wise precaution. China has one of the highest incidences of hepatitis-B, with about one-third of the world's infections occurring on the mainland. The country is also very conscious of the growth in HIV/AIDS cases since the first one was reported in 1985. Short-term visitors face no restrictions, but any foreigner wishing to work in the country for a Chinese organization has to undergo an HIV test in order to obtain a visa. Foreigners are seen as having a loose code of sexual morality and are often suspected of having sexually transmitted diseases.

Standards of care vary, and you would be well advised to take with you a supply of any medicines and pharmaceutical products you think you may need. Hypodermic needles, for instance, are often used more than once, so take some unused sterile needles with you in case you need to have an injection of some sort.

Chinese doctors will commonly want to give you an injection for even the most minor ailments, but you can always resist and request some other form of treatment. Sometimes prescription drugs that are no longer used in the West turn up in strange places, or  are prescribed for illnesses other than those for which they were originally developed. For example, one Western sufferer from asthma was prescribed Valium, commonly used as a tranquilizer. Make sure, before you leave home, that you have adequate insurance coverage, as medical care is not free. Western embassies are a good source of help, and in Beijing, Guangzhou (Canton), and Shanghai there are medical clinics set aside to help foreigners. If you have an accident, try to get a taxi to take you to an ordinary hospital. With the free-for-all commercial climate in China today, there's no knowing what may happen. One foreign visitor who broke his leg called the police to help him and was taken to a military hospital. There they put a cast on his leg and then tried to charge him 10,000 *renminbi* for the privilege— about one hundred times more than an ordinary hospital would have charged.

CHINESE MEDICINE

Traditional Chinese medicine is based on the understanding that the body is a cosmos in miniature, subject to the same forces of Yin and Yang that govern the universe, and that our health or illness is a reflection of harmony or disharmony in the flow of *qi* (which can be translated as "vital energy") through the whole organism. There are several Chinese systems of healing, of which acupuncture and herbal medicine are probably the two best known in the West. If you are offered a choice of Western or Chinese medicine, do not automatically feel you must choose the former. Acupuncture in particular (with sterile needles, of course) can be extremely effective for some conditions, as can some of the traditional herbal remedies.

Acupuncture has been practiced for at least two thousand years. According to the theory, one's health depends on having an uninterrupted flow of *qi*—if there is too little *qi*, or too much, or if its flow is obstructed in some way, symptoms will appear that require treatment. The treatment involves the insertion of thin stainless steel needles into energy points of the body where needling is thought to produce the

desired effects. The needles are then made to vibrate several hundred times a minute by connecting them to an electric current for a short time. It is especially helpful in relieving deepseated pain, rheumatism, swellings of the joints, and similar problems. It is also used, with mixed results, to help people to stop smoking.

Instead of needles, some acupuncturists sometimes use mustard seeds fixed with sticking plaster to particular points in the ear—you press them hard for a few seconds, three times a day, and the effect is said to be as beneficial as using needles. (A good compromise for needle-phobes!)

Some practitioners also perform moxibustion. This is the burning of moxa (mugwort) on the surface of the body for therapeutic reasons. The gently smoldering herbs are put into little glass or plastic cups, which are then stuck on to various parts of the body.

Herbal medicine is popular throughout the Chinese world, and even in the West you may have seen a Chinese medicine shop with its tiers of small drawers filled with the various esoteric and expensive ingredients (animal, vegetable, and mineral) that are called for in traditionally prescribed medicines.

The diagnostic techniques of the traditional Chinese doctor include taking the patient's pulse for several minutes; the speed and strength of the pulse are believed to indicate certain characteristic states of health. The medicine prescribed will usually involve a number of different substances that have to be simmered together for a long time and will usually taste horrible.

BELIEFS ABOUT HEALTH

Despite being at ease with the inevitability of their own mortality, the Chinese place great value on various foods, symbols, and rituals that prolong life. There are many symbols of longevity, such as the deer—the god of longevity is often pictured riding on a deer's back. A perfect, round peach is another symbol, often seen in folk art, as are the tortoise and the crane. The figure of the crane with its wings outspread and its leg uplifted is often used during funeral processions—it is thought to carry the dead person up to heaven. Noodles are often eaten on the day of someone's birthday, because their long strands are supposed to symbolize long life.

Many foods are believed to have medicinal properties: for example, shark's fin soup is thought to protect against cancer, and for almost every illness there is a list of special foods that will be given to the sick person by their family to help them recover. Some of these may seem quite strange to Westerners: for example, headaches are sometimes treated by heating fresh ginger in the fire and sticking thin slices of it onto the forehead. But the remedies seem to work for people who believe in them, and are the subject of serious study in the West. It is remarkable how the Chinese have retained knowledge of their traditional medicine, the Western equivalent of which has been almost totally lost, to be replaced by reliance on manufactured drugs.

QIGONG AND THE MARTIAL ARTS

Go out into the streets at first light in any city in China, and you will find row upon row of middle-aged and elderly people silently absorbed in their morning exercises, each going through the series of movements that make up the slow, intricate ballet of *qigong*. This ancient form of breath control is both a moving meditation and the spiritual underpinning of Chinese martial arts.

Qi, as we have seen, is the word that describes the life force; *qigong* is a series of exercises—combining movement, breathing, and visualization—that direct the flow of energy around the body so that it brings physical and

psychological benefits to the practitioner. Some take it to the point where they try to perform what are almost circus tricks, such as driving nails through boards with their bare hands. Others practice *qigong* to heal illness by a sort of "laying on of hands." Opinions about its value are almost as divided in China as they are in the West. The most popular aspect of this traditional practice and the related martial arts can be seen in the numerous *gongfu* films, mostly made in Hong Kong and Taiwan, one of which, *Crouching Tiger, Hidden Dragon*, was a surprise hit in the West.

BATHROOM HYGIENE
Although most Westerners visiting China will use Western-style hotels, where the bathrooms will be similar to those at home, it is quite likely that they will come across Chinese-style toilets when out and about on sightseeing trips, factory visits, or in ordinary Chinese offices or homes.

A Chinese lavatory consists of a porcelain trough set in the floor, over which one has to squat, feet on either side, facing the end where there is a kind of hood. There is usually no lavatory paper (remember to take some with you), and even if there is, the Chinese usually require you to throw it into a special bin after use rather than to flush it down the pan. (This seems to be partly because of the limitations of the sewage system, but also because the Chinese use what is euphemistically referred to as "night-soil" as fertilizer, and they do not want strands of paper spread all over their fields with it.) As a result, public toilets in China, and sometimes even the communal ones in hotels, have a very distinctive and unpleasant smell and are not places in which to linger. It is often not possible to wash one's hands afterward either, so carry a packet of moistened tissues or keep a small bottle of water in your pack. Another treat in store for women visitors is that in poorer places there are often no doors on the toilets, so privacy is non-existent. In remoter rural areas, where foreigners are still a novelty, you can find yourself the focus of an interested audience of local women.

FOOD & DRINK

THE IMPORTANCE OF FOOD IN CHINESE CULTURE

Most Westerners will have tasted and enjoyed Chinese food in various forms in their own countries, and may even have learned the delicate art of eating with chopsticks. But they may be less prepared for what the writer Colin Thubron memorably describes as the "passionate relationship" of the Chinese to food. Folk memories of famine are recent (the last were in the 1960s) and there are still many areas where people's diet is limited and poor. Refrigeration is more widespread now, but the Chinese almost never eat "ready meals"; food is freshly cooked for each meal, and fish, meat, and poultry are often killed only a short time before they are cooked. Shopping in the markets or shops is done with immense gusto and everything is prodded, shaken, sniffed, and thoroughly checked before being purchased.

It is debatable whether, in purely Western terms, the Chinese eat a "healthy" diet. They eat many vegetables, things are cooked fast so that the goodness is not destroyed, and people eat small quantities fairly frequently—"grazing," rather than eating huge meals at one sitting, which is one reason why they tend to be much slimmer than people in the increasingly obese West. On the other hand they use a large amount of the very salty MSG (monosodium glutamate, or taste powder) in their cooking, as well as sugar; and in some regions of China there is a high incidence of certain types of cancer, due to the overuse of pickling, the only way some vegetables can be preserved through the winter.

At any rate, the Western visitor will experience a fantastic range of different foods, some wonderful (dumplings, tofu, sweet and sour soup, Mongolian hotpot, and hundreds more treats), and some less to Western tastes, such as "hundred-year-old eggs" or donkey stew. If the Westerner is overwhelmed by a desire for more familiar food, these days help is at hand. In the bigger cities, though more rarely in the rural areas, there are plenty of fast-food outlets selling hamburgers and pizzas; there are some Italian, Indian, Japanese, Korean, and Mexican restaurants, and also newly opened supermarkets (mostly French) that sell the foods of which, in the past, homesick Westerners could only dream—for example, bread, cheese, milk, coffee, and real chocolate.

DIFFERENT REGIONAL CUISINES

Chinese local dishes are said to have four, eight, and ten culinary schools, depending on which authority is consulted. Canton, Shandong, Sichuan, and Yangzhou make up four of them: if you count Hunan, Fujian, Anhui, and Zhejiang, you have eight culinary schools; add in Beijing and Shanghai, and that makes ten. You should also try the Middle Eastern–type cooking of the Muslim minorities, such as the Hui and Uighur people, whose roadside stalls produce wonderful (and very cheap) lamb kebabs wrapped in naan bread with salad and hot spicy sauce. Here are a few pointers about some of the schools of cookery.

Cantonese Food

Cantonese cuisine adopts the good points of all other culinary schools, and its selection of ingredients is extensive. River food and seafood are widely used, as well as birds, rats, snakes, and insects. There is a saying that "The Cantonese will eat anything with wings, except a plane, and anything with four legs, except a table." Cantonese cuisine pays attention to the use of fresh ingredients and has unique cooking methods. Representative dishes are "three kinds of snake stewed," cat meat, snake soup, casserole mountain turtle, and crispy skin suckling pig.

Shandong Food

Shandong cuisine is dominated by seafood, reflecting its nature as a peninsula surrounded by the sea. Typical dishes include stewed sea cucumber with scallion, stewed snakehead eggs, sea slugs with crab ovum, Dezhou grilled chicken, and walnut kernel in cream soup.

Sichuan Food

Sichuan cuisine is renowned for its searingly hot, peppery flavor. The variety of tastes is summed up in the phrase "a hundred dishes with a hundred flavors." Famous dishes include shredded pork with fish flavor, stewed beancurd with minced pork in pepper sauce, and dry-roast rock carp. Those who are not used to extremely hot food should proceed with care. The Sichuanese use a special black pepper that leaves the lips numb—a bit frightening the first time it happens, but not unpleasant when one grows accustomed to it.

Huaiyang Food

Huaiyang cuisine integrates the cream of dishes in Yangzhou, Zhenjiang, Huaian, and other places south of the Yangtze River, stressing freshness and tenderness, careful preparation, cutting skill, bright color, beautiful arrangements, and light flavoring. Famous dishes include beggar's chicken, fried mandarin fish with sweet and sour sauce, sliced chicken with egg white, salted duck, steamed crab meat, and minced pork balls cooked in a casserole.

Vegetable Dishes

Vegetable dishes have been popular since the Song dynasty (960–1279) and they were greatly developed in the Ming and Qing dynasties (1368–1911). They were divided into three schools: Monastery Vegetable Dishes, Court Vegetable Dishes, and Folk Vegetable Dishes. The main features of vegetable dishes are their unique style and their health benefits. Main materials include green leaf vegetables, fruit, edible mushrooms, and beancurd products with vegetable oil as a condiment, all of which are delicious in taste, rich in nutrition, easy to digest, and believed to be helpful in preventing cancer.

JASMINE TEA AND HOT RICE WINE

The Chinese drink large quantities of tea (mostly green tea, as opposed to the black tea that is more commonly drunk in the West) and they add no milk or sugar. Tea is drunk constantly at meetings and at work, less so in restaurants and at formal meals, though it is always available if asked for. It is usually served in mugs with lids to keep it warm. Teabags and tea strainers are not used, and drinking tea without swallowing a mouthful of tea leaves requires concentration: try using the lid as a strainer when sipping.

Tea is divided into green, black, perfumed, white, and Wulong tea. The most valuable green teas are Longjing and Biluochun; black tea, Qihong and Yunfeng; scented tea, Jasmine; white tea, Yinzhenbaihao, Gongmei, and Shoumei; Wulong tea, Dahongpao and Tieguanyin. The Chinese will frequently give beautifully decorated tea caddies of special (and very expensive) teas as a present.

Other drinks you may be offered are yellow rice wine, served hot in little porcelain cups. It tastes rather like sherry. More lethal is *maotai*, the Chinese answer to vodka; there are also many light Chinese beers, as well as a growing range of Chinese wines—Great Wall wine is perhaps the best known and has improved considerably since the producers set up a joint venture with a French wine grower. Soft drinks such as mineral water and Coca Cola are available everywhere, and fruit juices made from the exotic tropical fruits grown in the south of China are delicious.

TEAHOUSE TRANQUILLITY

One interesting development since the late 1990s has been the reemergence of teahouses. Teahouses were traditionally the haunts of intellectuals and literati, who would idle away hours in stimulating conversation or in composing poems. In puritanical postliberation China, such establishments were considered a decadent remnant of the feudal society. But with the emergence of the five-day working week, and more emphasis on quality leisure time, the traditional teahouse is once again blossoming in major cities.

Teahouses have one thing in common: tranquillity—a precious commodity in China. The quiet atmosphere is broken only by leisurely music played on the *zheng,* a twenty-one- or twenty-five-stringed plucked instrument, in some ways similar to the zither. Conversation tends to be carried out in hushed tones. Teahouses are located at quiet places in beautiful surroundings, often near lakes: most cities have several now. The teahouse has its own slot on TV too—the British television company Granada has cooperated with Chinese TV to produce a 230-part soap called *Joy Luck Street*, based around the comings and goings in a teahouse; it was inspired by the long-running British TV soap *Coronation Street*, whose central location is a good old English pub.

SMOKERS' PARADISE

Cigarette smoking is widespread among men in China, much less so among women, and at formal meals cigarettes are almost always offered along with the tea. Most Chinese people do not seem to be at all worried about the links between smoking and health problems. It is very hard to escape from other people's cigarettes in restaurants. Young Chinese men set on having a good night out can even be seen holding a lit cigarette in one hand and a pair of chopsticks in the other—managing to smoke and eat at the same time. In theory smoking is now banned in various public places in China, as elesewhere in the world, but in practise it is still very common.

TIME OUT

GETTING AROUND
Two Feet
Going for a walk in the towns is a pleasure. Streets
in China are packed, and there is plenty to look
at—and plenty of people looking at you, with
your round eyes, funny hair, large nose, and
differently shaped body. The attention is not
hostile though, and a friendly smile will be
reciprocated with delight. As for walking in the
countryside, this is best done down in the
southwest, where there are mountains and
bamboo forests to wander through; paths are
marked and there are old Buddhist monasteries
and ancient little wayside inns to stay in.

Two Wheels
In towns, and in flatter parts of the countryside,
many foreigners hire bicycles to get around, and
this is highly recommended. Bikes need a good
sturdy padlock as they are frequently targets for
thieves (even though they have individual
registration numbers, just like cars). There are
plenty of places to park your bike, where, for a
small fee, a vigilant parking attendant will watch

over it. When you take charge of the bike, make sure that it works—dud brakes and loose pedals that fall off as you ride along are fairly common.

Disabled Access

Access for disabled visitors is not good, but attitudes are improving. Deng Puo Fang, one of the sons of Deng Xiao Ping, was confined to a wheelchair after Red Guards broke his back by pushing him out of a window during the bitter power struggles of the Cultural Revolution. He devoted the rest of his life to campaigning for better recognition and more help in China for people with a wide range of disabilities.

Flexible Rules

Individual Chinese can bend the rules and be very kind to visitors with disabilities. For instance, one blind American visitor to the Forbidden City was given a personal tour of the priceless antiquities there by the guide, who removed the ropes separating the exhibits from the crowds, took the man's hand and guided it over everything while describing it to him in detail.

Buses are impossible for wheelchairs, and trains also; disabled toilet facilities are almost unknown. As many deliveries to shops and offices are still made by carts and bicycles there are at least ramps up into many of the shops and other buildings. There are Web sites that give more information.

Tipping Is No Longer Taboo

Tipping used to be expressly forbidden in the PRC, and would be rejected if offered. The habit is now beginning to creep in, but should be resisted, or kept to reward exceptionally good service. Chinese taxi drivers will accept a tip if offered but will not expect one. If you are allocated a driver by the organization looking after you, he will be pleased if you offer him cigarettes. The person in charge of you will also make sure that he gets his meals and breaks and so on, so you do not have to worry about his welfare.

Taxis

The taxi service in most Chinese cities is excellent (another welcome change from the old days) and taxis are strictly metered and controlled. However, most taxi drivers speak no English, so it is advisable to ask someone in your hotel to write down your destination in Chinese so that you  can show it to the driver. You may occasionally find that a taxi driver refuses to take you in his cab. If this happens, it makes no sense to argue. One just has to be philosophical about it, as about many things in China that differ from home. Once you get into the cab, make sure that the driver starts the meter running, and remember to fasten your seat belt. Be warned—driving can be erratic and nerve-racking, especially if you are sitting in the front seat. Traffic accidents are very common.

Air Travel

China is a vast country and the quickest way to cover long distances is by air. The Chinese used to have a rather poor record on air safety for domestic flights, but this has now improved. However, be prepared for long delays with no explanations offered. Flying is relatively expensive and not as interesting as traveling by train.

Rail Travel

This is the way most Chinese people get around the country, but getting tickets can be extremely difficult and needs to be done well in advance of your trip. Your ticket is good for one train only, so do not miss it. Travel by train is not fast (not even the "express" trains), but it gives the traveler a much better idea of what China is like.

The rail network is huge and seems to be permanently overcrowded, especially at festival times when the whole of China is on the move, trying to get home to their families. You can travel "soft" class or "hard" class, but you may be expected, as a foreigner, to pay more than a Chinese person would.

Soft-class accommodation is very comfortable, with four berths in the sleeping compartments and air-conditioning. Hard-class sleepers are arranged in serried ranks in a sort of dormitory car, with no doors to separate the different sections: they are fairly comfortable, if totally lacking in privacy. Least comfortable, and certainly not to be recommended for journeys of more than a few hours, is hard-seat accommodation. This is usually dangerously overcrowded by Western standards, and, although providing an unparalleled insight into Chinese life, is not for the fainthearted.

There is usually no separate accommodation for nonsmokers, and Chinese men smoke incessantly to pass the time on long train journeys—sometimes they even smoke in the couchettes, in the middle of the night when everyone is trying to get some sleep. Another problem for anyone hoping to sleep on these journeys is that everyone snores, and if lying awake at home next to one snoring person has bothered you, just try a whole carriage full. The thin blankets that are handed out to the occupants of the hard-class couchettes are rather scratchy and can harbor some interesting specimens of insect life; avoid this by bringing your own blanket and some insecticide.

Bus Travel

It is possible to travel by long-distance bus in China, but again this is not very safe given the state of the roads and of the buses, nor very comfortable, especially if you are carrying a lot of baggage, which will be crammed around your knees.

Travel by Boat

Though crowded, this is also quite common and can be very enjoyable—there are regular boats along the Yangtze River, along the Grand Canal, and up the Pearl River from Canton (Guangzhou) to Wuzhou. (For more information on all these "journeys of a lifetime," there are suggestions for useful books at the end of this one.)

RULES AND REGULATIONS

Individual travelers wishing to make their own way can obtain a thirty-day tourist visa at any Chinese consulate or other organization overseas authorized by the Ministry of Foreign Affairs. For a party of more than four people a group visa can be obtained. Visitors wanting to stay beyond thirty days can usually gain an extension (up to sixty days) by applying to the local entry and departure administrative departments of the Public Security Bureau. The extension must be obtained prior to the expiry of the existing visa, and there is usually no problem with this.

Business travelers normally require an invitation letter from a recognized Chinese organization or enterprise in order to obtain a visa. Some business people circumvent this by entering on a tourist visa, but this can lead to problems.

Tourists visiting the PRC may wish to leave all the arrangements in the hands of the China Travel Service, which has offices in many countries. In that case, the CTS will arrange all the necessary visas, but the downside is likely to be a highly regimented program with little chance for improvisation.

Tibet

Tibet is now much more open to foreign visitors than in the past. But tourists need to obtain separate visas, after obtaining permission from the Tibet Tourism Administration or one of its overseas offices. Visitors should try to go there overland. Lhasa is 12,001 feet (3,658 meters) above sea level, and other parts of Tibet are even higher. Some travelers have experienced severe altitude sickness there, especially if they fly in. Arrival by train or bus gives the body more time to acclimatize.

"Sensitive Zones"

Holders of tourist visas must pass through Chinese ports designated as open to visitors from abroad. Although most of China is now open to foreigners there are still some places, particularly in sensitive border areas, that are restricted, and it is advisable to check this in advance. Travelers have been arrested and interrogated for entering these zones, and even expelled from the country. Foreigners visiting China on normal travel permits may not engage in activities that do not conform with their permitted status, such as taking up employment, study, or reporting. The authorities are particularly sensitive about journalists who sometimes masquerade as tourists in order to gain unsupervised access to strategic areas such as Tibet.

Taking Photos

Visits to temples, palaces, museums, and so on are straightforward and demand no special behavior. But remember that it is polite to ask permission before you take a photograph of a person (even though this may result in a request for a small payment). Photographers are not always welcome. In temples, be especially sensitive— there may be people worshiping—and try not to cause too much of a stir by your presence. Do not point your camera at policemen or at soldiers guarding government buildings, and be careful about taking pictures at airports. Railway stations are fine though, and if you like steam trains, China is the place to take your camera.

MONEY AND SAFETY

Gone are the days when foreigners had to pay for everything in FEC (Foreign Exchange Certificates, popularly known among Westerners as "funny money"). Nowadays, all cash transactions are in *renminbi* ("people's currency"), also known as the *yuan* (dollar), which is what you will be given when you change your money at the airport or at banks or hotels. (It is not possible to buy *renminbi* outside China, yet.) There are 1, 5, 10, 50, and 100 *yuan* notes. The *renminbi* is broken up into 100 *fen*, and there are coins of 1, 2, 5, and 10. To complicate things, the Chinese always refer to the 10 *fen* coin as either a *jiao* or a *mao*.

US dollars are much in demand, but remember that the illegal money-changers who accost you in the street, and who seem to be active all over China, could get you into serious trouble. Counterfeiting is a problem, and the likelihood of being given false 50 or 100 *yuan* notes is very high. Exchange rates seem to be much the same wherever you change money, so do not waste time shopping around. There are branches of many Western banks in Beijing now, but you should not have difficulty in changing travelers' checks or currency in branches of the Bank of China, or in your hotel. Keep the receipts of all your money-changing transactions to ensure that you have no problems changing the local currency back into your own when you leave the country, although this, too, is much less rigid than it was.

Credit cards, although increasingly widespread in use, are not yet as commonly acceptable in China as in the West, so you may want to carry more cash on you than you normally would. Watch out for pickpockets, however—also an increasingly widespread phenomenon. There are large numbers of unemployed people coming to the big cities, desperate for work; foreigners are known to be rich. Crime in China is still remarkably low, and many foreign visitors say they feel safer there than they would in the streets of New York or London: muggings and street crime are rare. But be sensible.

SHOPPING

Shopping is now seen as a patriotic duty as well as a popular leisure activity. With the advent of joint-venture shopping centers and a much freer market for consumer goods, the wind of competition has swept through China, and there is a much wider variety of goods available at a far larger number of outlets than used to be the case—so much so, that China is rapidly becoming a shopper's paradise. In the main cities, stores are usually open from 9:00 a.m. to 9:00 p.m. seven days a week, and in Shanghai until 10:00 p.m.

Street markets are another wonderful place to browse, with haggling all part of the fun. Even in the shops where, in theory, prices are fixed, there is often room for a bit of bargaining, especially as there is so much competition for custom now. In the markets it is normal for the price quoted to start at about three times the eventual price you can expect to pay. Chinese customers are very wary shoppers and to Western ears they sound quite rude—but sales staff are a robust bunch, unlike the sleepy, state-funded traders of old. Many are very astute young saleswomen (men are not a patch on them for persistence) from the poorer parts of China and will be insistent but not aggressive; they often know not only enough English to talk to customers, but also Russian, French, and German.

In a short space of time China has gone from a country with almost nothing to buy to a place that manufactures most of the clothes sold in Western shops, including designer-label stores; its factories also turn out hats, underwear, jewelry, handbags, backpacks, furniture, lighting, digital cameras, computers, cell phones, and televisions for the world market. Never mind bringing an extra bag home from China to carry all the shopping you have done there; soon you will have to hire a small truck!

What To Buy
Apart from clothes and other products made in China for export to the West and Japan, China's arts and crafts, reflect its long cultural traditions,

and they are flourishing. Carving, embroidery, pottery and porcelain, glassware, weaving, printing, wood carving and dyeing, and perfect replicas of ancient cultural relics are all exquisitely made by hand—labor is still cheap enough for this to be possible.

China's handmade carpets sell briskly on international markets. Some of the folk art is very attractive, too—patchwork for example, as well as folk scissor-cuts created by women farmers—and are all well worth seeking as gifts to take home.

The visitor should be careful about buying antiques. These should be bought at official stores, and will bear a special seal authorizing their export. China has lost enough antiquities one way and another in the past, and is now hanging on to what it has left. There is a bigger supply of legitimately available antiques in Hong Kong, where many were taken by families fleeing the turmoil of the 1930s and '40s There are, of course, very attractive fakes to be found as well.

NIGHTLIFE

Cities large and small in China used to settle down wearily for the night at around 8:00 p.m. Now they never sleep. There is an ever-increasing variety of entertainment and leisure activities available in China. Apart from cinemas, theaters, and food outlets (pizzas and burgers are all the rage), there are karaoke clubs, cyber cafés, MTV lounges, bars, and nightclubs, all ready to welcome you and help you spend some money. There are often a number of "hostesses" in these places, both Chinese and Western (especially young women from Russia). They tend to be heavily made-up and provocatively dressed—the puritanism of the past is long gone. Another legacy of the past that has vanished as is that of foreigners and Chinese being forced to sit in different parts of restaurants, stay in different hotels, shop in different shops, pay different prices, and so on. Bizarrely, it was probably the arrival in Beijing of the world's largest McDonald's in the 1990s that hastened the dismantling of the rule on separate restaurant seating for foreigners and Chinese—there was no way that the authorities could enforce it in a fast food outlet, and it just crumbled away.

CULTURE
Peking Opera

A uniquely Chinese form of entertainment is the Peking Opera. ("Peking" was the way foreigners used to pronounce what is now universally called "Beijing," or "northern capital city.") Peking Opera is a form of traditional Chinese drama that has been popular for about a hundred and fifty years, and involves acrobatics, fencing, and boxing, as well as music and singing. The music may sound harsh and discordant to the Western ear, but the whole thing is definitely a spectacle worth seeing. The actors wear elaborate costumes and colorful, stylized makeup. The audience is almost as interesting as the characters on stage. They will virtually all know the story of the opera by heart, and probably the music too: this means they feel free to get up and walk about during the performance, chat loudly to their friends, buy and eat snacks, and generally behave in a way quite diffcrent from the hushed, almost religious, stillness of opera audiences in the West.

Cinema
Chinese and foreign films are offered and ticket prices are cheap. Chinese film directors such as Chen Kai Ge and Zhang Yimou have won prizes and praise at foreign film festivals in recent years, with films such as *Yellow Earth* and *Raise the Red Lantern*, but in their home country, their brand of slow-moving "art house" films, beautifully shot in the Chinese countryside, and with a subtly critical social message, are much less popular than they are abroad.

Other Entertainments
The bigger cities not only offer ballet, theater, pop, and classical music concerts (again, with very cheap tickets compared to similar events in the West), but also art exhibitions and various sporting events. Check in the English-language magazines for current and forthcoming events. Outside the big cities, of course, things are a bit more limited.

chapter eight

BANQUETS & ENTERTAINING

Banquets are a regular feature of life for the business person visiting China, and for anybody whom the Chinese wish to welcome—visiting students, diplomats, filmmakers, academics, or overseas Chinese coming back to the ancestral home. Return hospitality may be expected, or it may be more appropriate to wait to invite the Chinese in your own country if they plan to visit you there.

THE GOOD GUEST
A banquet is one of the few occasions in China where having an idea in advance of the required behavior really does make a difference: it feels as though everyone has a scripted part, and it helps to know yours too. Evening engagements can be formal, so take smart evening wear. Behavior will be formal as well. One major difference with a Western-style meal or dinner party is that conversation will often be just between the most senior member of the Chinese organization and his (sometimes her) counterpart on the Western

side. Everyone else, more junior in rank, will tend to eat in silence, despite the Western visitor's wellmeaning attempts to get them to join in. This is worst at banquets with senior politicians, where sometimes the minister will do all the talking while his retinue limit themselves to showing their appreciation of the conversation (or the monologue). It can be a strain for the Westerner who ends up having to make all the conversation in return. Do not be surprised if people are too shy to chat back to you.

GREETINGS

Shake hands with everyone. Exchange business cards with people you may not have met yet. If you have brought gifts, leave the giving of them to the end of the meal. Tea and snacks may be offered before everyone sits at the table, or you may go to the table straight away.

SEATING AND TABLE ARRANGEMENTS

The Chinese host, who usually sits facing the door, will place the most eminent guest in the seat of honor to his right, and the deputy Chinese host will place the next most senior guest on his right, at the opposite side of the table. If

there is an interpreter, he/she will probably be seated to the right of the most important guest. Age and seniority are respected in the seating arrangements. Hosts and guests will normally be seated alternately around the table.

When you sit down, you are unlikely to find a knife and fork laid for you, so be prepared to try eating with chopsticks. Most foreigners manage to use chopsticks to convey the food to their mouths; very few ever master the knack of holding them properly, which Chinese children learn at their mother's knee. Asking for a demonstration from your hosts can be a good ice-breaker.

EATING

Banquets can consist of up to a dozen courses, sometimes even more, so pace yourself. In the north of China, soup is often served at the end of the meal, which will usually begin with a dish of cold hors d'oeuvres, but in the south of China soup may be served as the first course. The Chinese do not, as a rule, eat dessert, although fresh fruit may be provided. If there is any rice, it will not be served until near the end of the meal: it is seen as a "filler," in case the guests are still hungry, and therefore it is polite to leave some of it in your bowl, to show that you have been well fed and have no need of anything more.

Watch what the Chinese diners do when they help themselves to the communal dish of food—they may use a serving spoon, but it is very common to use one's own chopsticks. There may also be some "public chopsticks" (*gong kuaize*) that are used by everyone to serve themselves.

Do not be surprised if your host is continually placing the tastiest morsels on your plate—this is one way of honoring a guest, who should always wait to be urged to eat before helping himself. You may be given a hot, damp towel to wipe your hands

with. If it is given to you before the meal, you can use it as a napkin for the rest of the meal. If you find something in your mouth that you want to remove, use your chopsticks or the porcelain soupspoon, not your fingers. The Chinese themselves would spit it out, onto a little plate, so that, too, would be acceptable. Lifting your bowl (of soup, rice, and so on) so that it is closer to your mouth is not rude, and makes eating soup and rice much less hazardous.

Alcohol and Tea

Alcohol is very important for the drinking of toasts at banquets and formal meals, but most Chinese are not heavy drinkers and tend not to drink without food. You will probably find three glasses beside your plate, one for the very good lager-type beer that is commonly drunk and is not very strong, one for some kind of wine (either of the  Vermouth-type, or one of the rather sweet grape wines produced locally), and a small one for a more fiery liquor, such as *maotai,* which is distilled from sorghum and is 65–70 percent proof. The *maotai* is usually used for toasts, and you will often see the Chinese finish off a whole glass each time (but they are very small glasses).

MAKING SPEECHES AND PROPOSING TOASTS

Speeches, which always end with one side toasting the other, usually happen quite soon after the beginning of the meal. The host will probably speak between the arrival of the first and second dishes, and the chief guest should reply a few minutes later, after the start of the second dish. Take a lead from your host and keep your speech short and fairly bland. Make a few general appreciative comments about your visit, some remarks about hopes for future cooperation, friendly ties between your organizations, and so on—and, above all, avoid elaborate jokes as they are often untranslatable, or at least no longer funny once they have been translated.

Don't Joke!

A Canadian journalist writes of how he had once been present at a grand banquet in the Great Hall of the People in Beijing. During the speeches, a visiting diplomat embarked upon a long and complicated joke in English. The poor Chinese interpreter, having tried in vain to translate it, finally despaired. He simply said, in Chinese, "The honored foreign visitor has just told a joke— please laugh!" The audience obliged and face was saved all round.

Cheers!

At the end of the toast, the proposer says "Cheers!" The Chinese equivalent of "Cheers" is "*ganbei*" (literally, "dry glasses"), but caution is advisable here because there will often be a number of toasts to follow. However, the consumption of large amounts of alcohol at banquets and other celebratory events is being officially discouraged.

If you do not want to drink alcohol, soft drinks (Coca Cola or fizzy orange squash), green tea, and mineral water will be available.

MAKING POLITE CONVERSATION

If you find that the atmosphere at the banquet is not too formal, make the effort to talk to your Chinese hosts, rather than spend the entire time chatting to your Western colleagues. Talking to your hosts may seem difficult to begin with, but is very rewarding. Food is one good topic of conversation, and the discussion of the relative merits of different places in China is another. Don't talk about religion, bureaucracy, politics, Tibet, Taiwan, or sex. Lightweight topics such as holidays, tourism, travel, and plans for the future are fine, and you can talk about families too.

THE RETURN MATCH

If you decide to arrange a return banquet for your Chinese hosts before you leave, ask your interpreter, or whoever is organizing your visit, to help you. A table plan should be drawn up, and at the banquet there should be place cards. A supply of foreign cigarettes is always welcome on such occasions. Remember that as host it will be your job to keep plying your guests with food, and other people in your organization can do likewise, especially each time a new dish arrives. Your guests will be loath to help themselves and will often decline something offered to them several times before they feel able to accept, so you will have to keep pressing them to eat. It is hard work being a host and a guest at a Chinese banquet, but they are rewarding occasions nonetheless.

A Change of Style

Perhaps the very formal banquet has had its day. When the then American President George W. Bush visited Beijing in February 2002, Western rather than Chinese food was served at the welcoming banquet. In another break with tradition, as the banquet came to an end, in place of the usual hasty farewells an accordionist appeared, and Bush's host, the then President Jiang Zemin, serenaded the Americans with a rendering of "*O sole mio.*"

chapter nine

BUSINESS BRIEFING

CHINA'S ENTRY TO THE WORLD TRADE ORGANIZATION

China's entry to the World Trade Organization (WTO) in 2001 was a highly significant event in her long history. The WTO is the only global international organization dealing with the rules of trade between nations: it is a forum in which the one-hundred-and-forty-plus member states can negotiate trade relations and terms. At its heart are the WTO agreements, negotiated and signed by the majority of the world's trading nations and ratified in their parliaments. The WTO's predecessor, the General Agreement on Tariffs and Trade (GATT), was a provisional organization established in 1947. In 1994 the GATT was turned into the permanent WTO.

The WTO aims at reducing tariffs and nontariff trade barriers (such as quotas) between member states. In order to do this, a member state must treat the goods and investments coming from other member states on the same terms as its own, and the rights enjoyed by one member state must be extended to all other member states.

China was one of the twenty-three original signatories of the GATT in 1948. After the revolution in 1949, the Nationalist government in Taiwan announced that China would leave the GATT system. Although the Beijing government never recognized this decision, nearly forty years later, in 1986, it notified the GATT of its wish to resume its status as a GATT contracting party.

Reversing the tradition of decades of employing Party members whose knowledge of (and interest in) the outside world was sketchy to say the least, China has given its civil servants and those working in enterprise ("enterprise executives") special training on WTO rules. And, rather reluctantly, thousands of officials are starting to learn English, as the government feels they should be capable of handling the expected vast increase in international communications.

For the member states of the WTO, China offers a huge potential market for investment and sales. But what does China get out of it? China's reasons for joining are to enable it to enjoy the various rights available to other member states, and to have a say on international trade matters. Some economists predicted that in the short run, with the expected surge of imports and increased competition, inefficient domestic enterprises would be forced to reform or shut down, which could lead to higher unemployment. However, in the long run, they predicted increased productivity, inflow of foreign capital, and transfer of technology and expertise.

The official view, given in President Jiang Zemin's speech in 2001, is that joining the WTO "is a strategic decision made by the Chinese Government under economic globalization and is in line with China's reform and opening-up policy and the goal of establishing a socialist market economic system. The efforts made by China for its WTO accession have greatly accelerated the reform and opening-up process in China."

THE BUSINESS CULTURE

These days, there is a new confidence and pride in China, and Westerners should be very careful not to behave in a superior manner, or expect to rush things through. Things in China will proceed at the pace they wish them to— which is usually quite slow. Those Chinese who deal with foreigners are very aware of China's attraction for potential business partners, but they are also very knowledgeable about technology, international pricing, and world markets.

Your Hosts

After your arrival in China, any arrangements for your travel within the country will usually be taken care of by the organization you are visiting. You will probably be met by representatives of the organization when you arrive, whether at the airport or the railway station, and you will also probably be seen off by them when you leave. More senior members of the organization are likely to say goodbye to you at your hotel, while relatively junior members will escort you all the way to your point of departure. This is the custom in China, and you should do the same for your guests.

Greeting People

Make sure to shake hands with everyone in the group—it is impolite to shake hands with only the first few and then give up. You will no doubt notice that there is no custom of giving precedence to the female members of the group. The Chinese incline their heads a little on meeting someone new, but there is none of the elaborate bowing that characterizes Japanese culture.

Seniority Counts

The Chinese are very status conscious, so it is best to remember, when dealing with a group, that they will come into the room in order of seniority. However, the actual negotiations may be carried out by someone other than the most senior member. This may be because the most senior person is a more of a figurehead, whereas someone more junior may well have studied abroad and received an MBA at an American or other foreign university.

Business Cards

When you go to a business meeting, the first thing that happens is an exchange of business cards. When someone hands you his or her card, make sure to read it, not just glance at it and put it away. You may well find it helpful to place the cards you receive on the table in front of you, to remind yourself of the names and titles of your Chinese counterparts.

It is a good idea to take along a large stock of business cards, if possible with a Chinese version of your name, your company's name, and your job title on the back. (See the section on names, page 75.) If you do not have time to get the cards made locally, you can probably have them printed in your own local "Chinatown," or else in Hong Kong if you are passing through there; or after you get to China you can ask the reception desk in your hotel for help in finding a reliable printer. You should also take with you an indexed cardholder of some sort to keep the cards organized, as you will collect a great many of them.

Whoever chooses your Chinese name should keep it to two or three syllables—anything longer could be difficult for the Chinese to manage. And remember that the simplified forms of the Chinese characters that are now in use in the PRC are not normally used in Taiwan or Hong Kong. Check this when you order your cards from the printer.

What to Wear
Dress should be quite formal. For men, suits and ties are best, with lightweight ones for the hotter, southern parts of China, or summer in the north.

It is quite acceptable for women to wear trousers, as most Chinese women do, but skirts or suits are widely perceived as smarter. Bare legs, even on the hottest summer day, are out for women. They should dress modestly (no sundresses or low necklines, for example), and should not behave in too extroverted a manner. "Loud" behavior or attention-seeking in either sex does not go over well in China. Banquets, as we have seen, may call for slightly more formal wear, so take something extra smart. After years of dressing down, younger Chinese women in particular are enjoying dressing up again, often in traditional Chinese clothes made in bright colors with much embroidery. Older women (thirty-five plus) tend to dress more soberly and to shun bright colors in favor of darker ones.

Women in Business

Foreign businesswomen visiting China will have no occasion to feel ill at ease simply because they are female. There may not be equal numbers of men and women in all occupations or at all levels in China, but there are, in theory at any rate, equal opportunities for both sexes, and the Chinese are quite happy to deal with both men and women, in business or as tourists.

Women who frequently visit the PRC on business report that they are well accepted by their male Chinese counterparts, and that it is not considered odd if they reciprocate toasts at banquets and so on.

Although most business entertaining is done in restaurants, it is not usual for spouses to be invited along. If your spouse happens to be in China with you, she/he can expect to have to amuse herself/himself on the evenings when there are banquets and so on, unless specifically included in the invitation.

Be on Time
Punctuality is considered very important when doing business in China. The people with whom you are dealing will not keep you waiting, and you should make a point of being on time too. Equally, it is important that you should not keep looking at your watch and implying that you are in a great hurry to finish a deal.

CONTACTING PEOPLE

Everyone you are likely to need to contact is bound to have access to e-mail now. E-mail and the Internet have revolutionized the possibilities for doing business or keeping in touch with China. The time difference with the USA, Europe, and Australia used to mean that phoning China was difficult, expensive, and unsatisfying. E-mails also fit better with the Chinese style of negotiating, as an e-mail allows someone time to reflect before they answer. It also means that individuals are more empowered than they were, now that many employees have PCs and are free to correspond directly with their Western contacts, rather than go through layers of bureaucracy. Getting to the right person initially may still take a while, but once you have your contact, things are much quicker.

The Cell Phone Revolution

The cell phone is another extraordinary success story in China. Until the mid-1990s, it was quicker to take a taxi across Beijing or Shanghai than to get through to someone on the telephone. In the days when only landlines were on offer, the Chinese had no choice but to share phones—the residents of a whole apartment block would have one telephone between them, privacy was out of the question, getting though to the person you wanted could take ages and when you did, the sound quality was terrible. At work, people tended to use the office phone to make all the calls they could not make from home—so no one could ever get through to workplaces either. Things were made worse by the Chinese fear of catching TB from the mouthpiece of a shared phone; as a result, people often put handkerchiefs over the mouthpiece, making it even harder to hear the conversation. Telephone directories were almost unknown (as were street maps); this was due to the obsession with secrecy that characterized the 1960s and 1970s, and to a lack of investment in modern telecommunications infrastructure. Even now, landlines are still not as popular in China as cell phones.

But the introduction of the cell phone has had an enormous impact on every aspect of life. Xinhua, the official Chinese news agency, estimated that there were 592 million users of cell phones in China in 2008. One out of every two SMS (text messages) sent in the world are sent in China. The cost is cheap—about 1 US cent for an SMS, and not much more for calls.

Of all the extraordinary changes in China since Mao died, the rise in the use of cell phones has probably made the greatest contribution to individual freedom. An article by Edward Cody in the *Washington Post* of June 2007 describes how, in the beautiful southern coastal city of Xiamen, protesters armed only with cell phones brought 10,000 people out on to the streets to campaign against a proposed chemical plant. As the police attempted to stop the march, the organizers sent text messages and photos to bloggers in nearby Guangzhou, who instantly posted them on the Internet. Traditional journalists covering the protests were afraid to report on it, but this inspired use of new technology jumped straight over the censors and led to a national debate about the proposed plant. Less political, but equally important for individual freedom, are the stories in the Chinese press of people able to carry on love affairs, illicit and otherwise, on a cell phone used only for that purpose. So it is hardly surprising that cell phone ettiquette dictates that everything stops when the phone rings, even more so than in the West.

Visitors can buy local SIM cards and put them into their own (unlocked) phones, or buy secondhand phones and SIM cards from tiny shops in the back streets of cities; but take a Chinese person with you on the shopping trip, as there are traps for the unwary—some very cheap SIM cards do not have the infrastructure to support them and hence only work in a few places.

Be Prepared for Interruption

The author of this book gave a lecture in Shanghai to an audience of nine hundred students, which was punctuated throughout by an equal number of phones, all ringing loudly. This is not considered rude in China, in the same way perhaps that talking during Peking opera performances is all part of enjoying the experience. But equally, it would not be rude of the foreigner who is about to give a presentation, to ask the audience (politely of course) if they would switch off their phones. Westerners are perhaps less able to cope with the distractions of constant noise than the Chinese.

NEGOTIATING TECHNIQUES

For readers interested in the practicalities of setting up a business in China there is a list of useful books and Web sites at the end. Here we focus on the cultural and social side of business dealings and of other professional relationships, such as those involving scientists or researchers.

When "No" Means "Maybe"

When in a professional relationship, a Chinese person may feel that a direct "no" would be embarrassing to both parties, and will try to convey disagreement by more indirect methods, such as evading the question or remaining silent. The Westerner needs to be sensitive to this, and learn to interpret the signals that his or her Chinese counterpart is giving out. In some cases, of course, what appears to be an attempt at stalling may genuinely mean that the person you are dealing with has to consult his superiors; in other cases it may be a sign that concessions on your part are required if the discussions are to go much further.

Requests for "commissions" and other forms of under-the-table payments are likely to be made indirectly. If the request is direct, rejection can be phrased in terms of "My country makes such payments illegal and my organization would be in big trouble if it agreed to this." There are other ways of equalizing the give and take on both sides—for many Chinese, the chance of a trip to the West to see how your organization does things and to travel a little is the greatest of any reward. But do not promise what you cannot deliver: a British TV producer on his first trip to Beijing promised an internship in London to the son of a professor who had helped him. Unfortunately, on his return to the UK, he found that the British government would not grant the young man a visa. The Chinese with whom you are dealing will tend to assume that you are powerful—otherwise your organization would not have sent you—and that you have the power to do what you promise. So if you are not sure what you can achieve for them, say so.

Acceptable Outcomes
Westerners tend to expect results from meetings, even if it is just an action plan, an agreement to meet again, rather than a decision. Minutes of the meeting

are taken to provide a record of what is said. Chinese meetings are less likely to lead to any result, at least not so quickly. They are an opportunity for people to state a position, which they will have decided in advance. There is rarely an agenda. There is a strict observance of rank as to who actually does the talking, and interrupting is considered rude. In the more modern, go-ahead companies things are changing fast, and meetings will more closely resemble the free-for-all, give and take, that Westerners are used to. But officialdom in China is slow to change and so are the longer-established organizations.

Preparation

If you prepare properly and well in advance for a meeting in China, it will work better for all concerned. Paperwork about your organization, your plans, and your project will have been read and discussed with a care and thoughtfulness that many Western managers can only dream of! It is better to come with a clear set of objectives, which each side has had time to think about, than to use the meeting as a sort of brainstorming session in the way that Westerners sometimes tend to.

Final Decisions May Not Be Final

Be prepared for the Chinese side to request changes to a contract even after it has been signed. Long-term relationships are more important than quick deals. It can take a long time for a contract to be signed. If you can get it translated into Chinese at your end, this will speed things up a bit.

BUSINESS COMMUNICATION STYLES

Here is a summary of the traditional cultural expectations each side brings to the relationship. But as China engages more with the West, things are changing.

USE OF NAME

Western: Tend to use first names on first meeting.

Chinese: More formal; use titles such as Mr. or Miss, or Mayor, Manager, Professor.

USE OF HUMOR

Western: Tell jokes and use humor as an icebreaker.

Chinese: Very sparing use of humor on first meeting—except for a carefully planned joke.

INTERRUPTIONS

Western: Feel free to interrupt the speaker and put their own point of view. Colleagues are geared up to respond to the body language of the person who wants to interrupt.

Chinese: Interrupting would be rude—unless it is done by a cell phone! More junior staff often pop in unannouced to the meeting and whisper messages to the boss—often these are about arrangements for lunch or other plans concerning the visitor. It is not rude to whisper to a colleague while someone else is speaking.

MAKING SURE YOU ARE UNDERSTOOD

Western: It is usual to structure presentations and to recap what has been said. It is normal to ask for clarification if necessary. The speaker is to blame if something is not as clear as it should be.

Chinese: Being clearly understood is not a priority, perhaps because at school they are used to listening in silence to the teacher. Saying "I don't understand" is a possible loss of face.

ARGUMENT VS. AGREEMENT

Western: People expect to argue things through and enjoy doing so. It is not rude to be adversarial. This is often the way to get noticed and promoted.

Chinese: The Chinese can be very argumentative among themselves, but this is unlikely to be displayed in front of a foreigner, even when they know and trust him or her.

ATTENTION SPAN

Western: Short, and getting shorter. Westerners tend to assume that people will be bored and try to come to the point quickly.

Chinese: Longer. The Chinese are trained from early childhood to listen politely and patiently. They do not come to the point quickly—to do so would be rude. You may not hear the information you have been waiting for until the meeting is almost over.

EYE CONTACT

Western: Too much eye contact makes people uneasy. Too little and they distrust you.

Chinese: Keep eye contact with your interlocutor. People who avoid eye contact are not considered trustworthy.

PRAISE

Western: Politeness and praise are important, but too much is seen as flattery and is mistrusted.

Chinese: Flattery is part of the negotiating process. It is given by praising people in front of their peers, and by expressing deference to superiors. This is part of "giving face" to someone; the opposite, making someone "lose face" by openly criticizing them, losing your temper with them, or deriding their point of view, is very rude indeed and is completely counterproductive.

SELF- DEPRECATION

Western: In Britain this is used a lot, less so in the USA.

Chinese: Individuals rarely criticize themselves, but will criticize their organization in a self-deprecating way, or say that things are very backward in China.

GETTING THINGS DONE

Western: Orders and instructions, even if given in a friendly manner, are direct. They can be questioned.

Chinese: Orders are given more indirectly, but compliance is expected. Instructions may be vague (this is a safety net), but carry authority.

WORK IN CHINA
Working Hours and Vacations

The Chinese get to work very early, but are not the most efficient users of time. They have a saying: "In the West, you waste everything except time; in China [where everything is recycled] we waste nothing except time." In the state sector and even in the private sector, staffing levels are high and people often do not have enough to do. Regular meal breaks punctuate the day—lunch is early, often at 12 noon, and in the hot weather many will take a siesta after lunch (the Chinese word is *xiuxi*, meaning rest). People go home around 4:00 or 5:00 p.m., and working late is rare, especially as public transport and roads are crowded and people have long, tiring journeys home.

In the days of Mao, holidays were almost unknown. Nowadays, paid holidays are becoming more widespread, especially at Chinese New Year (February), Labor Day (May 1), and National Day (October 1). A week off for one or all of these national holidays is intended to encourage the Chinese, by nature used to saving their money, to go out and get the economy moving by spending it in the shops and restaurants (and perhaps to feel that these patriotic days are a lot more fun than they used to be). It seems to have been a successful move.

Academic holidays are similar to those in the West, with the notable exception that there is no Christmas break. The school year begins in September. Students have their winter holidays from mid-January to the end of February, and their summer holidays from mid-July to the end of August. The dates of the winter holiday are set each year, as the Spring Festival is not fixed.

As we have seen, punctuality is important. However, once you have arrived, there is less of a rush than in the frantically busy West. Working patterns differ from the West; for example,Western film producers who are used to their film crews working a ten-hour day when making a TV program find that the Chinese crews put in about five hours a day, by the time lunch and various rest periods are taken into account. On the other hand, discuss and negotiate with your Chinese partners; if they know what you expect and need from them they will always try to accommodate you. Ironically there are no trade union regulations in China; health and safety rules are very lax and, for better or for worse, each contract is more or less up to the individual organizations involved.

Getting a Job in China

There are numerous possibilities now, and you do not even have to arrange a job before you go, though you will have to change the status of your visa. Working in China is one of the best ways to get to know the country and the people, as your status changes from an outsider who is just there to have fun to that of a fellow worker who is trying to help make the country propserous.

chapter ten

COMMUNICATING

MANDARIN, CANTONESE, AND OTHER FORMS OF CHINESE

Because of China's geography, transport and communications have always been difficult, so it is not surprising that over the course of her history, many different forms of the Chinese language have developed. These are usually referred to as "dialects," but since they are in many cases mutually unintelligible, it is more helpful to think of them as separate languages. There are eight major dialects, including Mandarin, Cantonese, Shanghai, Hakka, Amoy, Fuzhou, and Wenzhou, and many minor regional variations.

Mandarin is the official language used in both the PRC and Taiwan as the medium of education, and is the common means of communication in China. In the PRC it is called *putonghua* (common or standard speech), as well as *hanyu* (the language of the *han* people) and *zhongwen* (Chinese). In Taiwan it is known as *guoyu* (national language) or *huayu*. In theory, anyone under about fifty-five should be able to speak Mandarin—even if they prefer to speak their own local variety of Chinese at home—but in practice this is not always the case.

Strong local accents can make it hard to understand Mandarin spoken in more remote areas, or by less educated people—even the Chinese interpreter may have trouble. Another problem is that speakers of some Chinese dialects lack the sounds "r" and "n." So to the west of Beijing, the phrase "*Ni shi neiguo ren?*" or "What country are you from?" would be pronounced "*Li shi leiguo len?*" with the sound "l" substituted for both the initial "n" and "r." This is what led to the old Western caricature, at the beginning of the last century, of Chinese immigrants saying "flied lice" instead of "fried rice."

Chinese is a tone language, part of the Sino-Tibetan family of languages. English, by contrast, belongs to the Indo-European family. As a foreigner trying to speak Chinese, you are likely to have far more trouble with tones than with individual sounds. Chinese has fewer sounds than some other languages; and as English has more sounds, there are few actual Chinese sounds that pose problems for English speakers. Most Chinese words are made up of one syllable. Each syllable is represented by a single Chinese character. Some other south Asian languages work in the same way as Chinese, though with different written forms: Vietnamese, Burmese, and Thai, for example.

Tone languages are those in which a variation in the pitch of the voice in which a particular syllable is pronounced conveys differences in meaning. For example, *tang* said in a high level tone means "soup," but *tang* said in a rising tone means "sugar"; *gou* said in a fall-rise tone means "dog," but *gou* said with a falling tone means "enough."

There are four tones in Mandarin:

> level (and relatively high)
> rising
> fall-rise
> falling

This may sound complicated, but compared to other dialects—for example, Cantonese, which may have up to nine tones—it is fairly simple. Foreigners are often described as "tone deaf," as they have trouble even *hearing* the different tones, never mind reproducing them. Tones need a good deal of practice but, as with using chopsticks, if you ask your Chinese contacts to help you improve your pronunciation, this can be a useful conversational gambit. You still won't get it right, but your hosts can have a lot of fun helping you. Do not despair, however. As with any language, learning does *not* consist of repeating isolated words devoid of context. Learning some simple phrases is quite easy. Any minor difficulty you may have in learning these phrases will be far outweighed by the positive reaction you will get from Chinese people, and the context, as well as the willingness of your hosts to try and respond to your efforts, will help understanding.

Understanding Chinese English
The same is not true the other way around. According to the author Jung Chang: "In general,

Chinese speakers find English hard to pronounce and have trouble learning to understand the spoken language." She points out how one of the features that English speakers notice about the Chinese is the difficulty they have with what linguists call "reduced syllables." Chinese speakers tend to stress too many syllables. For example, they find it hard to say, as an English speaker would, "fish'n'chips," and will either say "fish and chips," or just "fish chips." The Chinese tend to separate the syllables of English words, and also the words themselves, as they would in Chinese. This leads to a sort of machine-gun effect when they speak English (especially among Cantonese speakers), rather than the smooth but varied "stream" effect that English should give. Combined with the fact that "please," "thank you," and "sorry" are not used nearly as often in Chinese as in English, this may lead to a perception of rudeness.

Pidgin English

The word "*pidgin*" (pronounced "pigeon," like the bird) comes from early Chinese attempts to pronounce the word "business." When traders from the USA, Britain, and Portugal visited the coasts of China in the early 1800s they found that understanding each other's language was a long and tedious process. Pidgin English, consisting of a few hundred English words, grew up as a way of filling this linguistic vacuum. The words were not used grammatically, and they popped up in Chinese sentence structures with Chinese pronunciation. The blend was made richer by the addition of some words of Hindi and Urdu, brought over by traders who had worked with the East India Company. After the Communists gained power in 1949, pidgin died out as it carried too much of the baggage of colonialism, but until then it was not only used as a way for foreigners and Chinese to communicate, but also for speakers of different Chinese dialects to talk to each other, before *putonghua* took over that role.

Picturesque words from those days survive in a few comic book stories such as *TinTin*, words like "*chop chop*," meaning hurry up. "*Chop*" on its own meant a trademark, brand, or name. Another one which survives is "*joss*" (as in joss-stick, a stick of incense), which comes from the Portuguese word "*deos*" (God), and means idol, god, or luck; from this comes the wonderful "*joss-pidgin-man*," or "god business man"—better known as a priest. Anyone fascinated by pidgin and other hybrid languages used by opium traders and sailors of the 1800s should read Indian author Amitav Ghosh's wonderful novel *Sea of Poppies*.

PINYIN: THE ROMANIZATION OF CHINESE CHARACTERS

The system of transliteration used in this book, Pinyin, was adopted by the PRC in 1979. The system it replaced was called Wade-Giles, named after its inventors. This is why it can be confusing to read books written some years ago with differently Romanized versions of Chinese place-names, such as Soochow, now written Suzhou. Add to that differences in regional accents, changes in place-names over time, and the Chinese habit of giving Chinese place-names to everywhere (such as Kashi for the northwestern town of Kashgar), and it is a wonder anyone gets anywhere. There are also places in the south of China that Westerners call by a version of their Cantonese name. For example, Hong Kong is known to Mandarin speakers (about 70 percent of China) by its Mandarin name, Xiang Gang or "Fragrant Harbor."

Nevertheless, the standardization that Pinyin has provided for the Chinese language is immensely useful. For example, telephone directories and dictionaries use Pinyin; as Chinese does not have an alphabet, this is the only way to put the information into alphabetical order. Chinese computer keyboards and cell phones use Pinyin. For example, if you type in the word *ma*, using the two letters of the Roman alphabet *m* and *a*, the screen gives you a choice of the many

different Chinese characters that can be used to write "*ma*" depending on its meaning. You just click on the correct character.

The Sounds of Pinyin

You cannot automatically give the letters used in Pinyin their usual sounds. Many do approximate to English sounds, but there are a number of conventions that have to be observed.

• **c** is pronounced as *ts* in "cats"
• **z** is pronounced as *ds* in "seeds"
• **q** is pronounced as *ch* in "cheap"
• **j** is pronounced as *j* in "jig"
• **x** is pronounced as something between *sh* in "shin" and *s*
• **s** as in "siesta"
• **r** is pronounced as a cross between *s* in "vision" and *r* in "red"
• **h** is pronounced as *ch* in Scottish "loch"
• **zh** is pronounced as *j* in "July"
• **a** is like *ar* in "far"
• **-ang** is like *ung* in Southern English "sung"
• **e** is like *er* in "her"
• **en** is like *en* in "stricken"
• **ei** is like *ay* in "hay"
• **ou** is like *ou* in "soul"
• **i** is like *ee* in "see," except after c, s, z, r, ch, sh, and zh, when it is like the *i* in American "sir"
• **u** is like *oo* in "soon"
• **ï** is like *e* in "see" but said with the lips rounded as if for "oo"
• **-ong** is like ung in German "Jung"
• **-ian** is like "yen"
• **ui** is like "way"

WRITTEN CHINESE

Early Chinese writing was based on pictograms that evolved into characters formed by a series of brush strokes. Chinese is believed to be among the world's oldest and continuously used written languages. Many Chinese characters have been traced back to the Shang dynasty, about 1500 BCE. Some Chinese characters still look like their origins, just simple pictures of the things they represent. Sun (*taiyang*) was a circle with a dot in the middle; now it is written like a box with a line across it. Water (*shui*) is three flowing lines; the character for a human (*ren*) looks like a little person with two legs (but no head). These simple concepts can be combined to make new ones; the characters for sun and moon together make the character for "bright." The character for "family" is made by putting the one for "roof" over the one for "pig."

Written Chinese is largely uniform throughout the country, although many of the characters are now written in a simplified form. In Hong Kong (for the time being) and Taiwan and other overseas Chinese communities the older, more complex form of the Chinese characters is used.

Estimates of the number of characters vary—but there are probably about 50,000. A working knowledge of a mere 3,000 gives you mastery of most menus and street signs; if you want to read the newspapers you will need about 7,000.

Most Chinese characters consist of two parts: the *radical*, which shows to which class the word belongs, and the *phonetic*, which tells how it is pronounced. For example, the character for pure, or clear, *qing*, has two parts; the water radical and the part which gives the pronunciation, *qing*.

清　⼀⼀　氵　water radical
　　　　　　　(word category)

　　　　　　青　phonetic element
　　　　　　　(pronunciation)

There are about 250 radicals, some quite common, such as the one used for anything concerned with fire, others more unusual.

The study of Chinese language and literature can become a lifelong interest. The Chinese government has recently started opening Confucius centers in countries such as the USA, Russia, and the UK for anyone interested in learning Chinese. Although learning Chinese characters appears a nightmarish task to Westerners, Chinese children start young and work very hard at it; illiteracy rates are low, though of course the number of characters a person knows depends on their educational level and on their job. The Chinese find the alphabetic script of Western languages difficult to decode. As Jung Chang puts it, ". . . the way the information is spread out in each word seems cumbersome for a reader used to the compact ideograms of Chinese."

One of the problems with each character being different (although the radicals give a clue, they can have a fairly loose connection with the actual meaning of the word) is that it is possible for the Chinese to come across a word they have never seen before in the newspapers or a book and not to know how to pronounce it. An example of this was the occasion when a foreign teacher in Beijing wanted to buy a dice (die) for her students to play (educational!) board games during lessons. Not surprisingly, given the Chinese love of gambling, everyone knew the *word* for this object, but no one knew how to write it down so that the teacher could show it to the shop assistants—possibly because under Mao gambling had been forbidden for decades. Eventually a very old man was found who knew how to write it. It turned out to have a bone radical, as in the days before plastic that was what dice were made of—but even when he wrote the character down, none of the young shop assistants could read it!

For foreigners, knowledge of a few Chinese characters is useful (exit, entrance, toilet, and so on) but not as necessary as knowledge of the spoken language. Many signs in big cities are now written in Pinyin to help the foreigner, as are road signs, because many foreign residents have their own cars. Some are even written in English. But outside the big cities signs in Pinyin or English are rare.

CALLIGRAPHY

Chinese people love to hang calligraphy on their walls—exquisitely painted Chinese characters that are either famous poems, mostly from the Tang dynasty, or well-known sayings. The art of the calligrapher is as appreciated as the art of the

painter, and people can recognize who has written/painted the characters in the same way that a Westerner can spot a Picasso or a Monet painting. Because characters are considered lovely in themselves, over the centuries some famous Chinese paintings and scrolls have had beautifully penned characters added to them by well known artists, usually expressing their appreciation of the picture. These are thought to add to their value. There is no Western equivalent to this: it would be as though a painting by Rembrandt had messages of critical acclaim from Cézanne and other painters scribbled down the side, which added another million dollars or two to its value at auction.

Another great difference is that where Western art and indeed most cultures prize originality above everything (sometimes seemingly above the actual quality of the art), Chinese art for centuries stuck firmly to the Confucian principle of constantly recreating the golden age of the past; techniques were learned (and still are) so that the pupil could paint in exactly the same way that the masters had painted several hundred years before he was born, and the subjects (bamboo, plum blossom, and so on) also never changed. Young Chinese painters have broken away from this tradition; the combination of more political freedom and a strong market for Chinese art, driven primarily by Chinese who have made money and want to invest in their own culture, have seen modern art flourishing in China. As always, the pragmatic goes hand in hand with the political.

Appendix: Simple Vocabulary

Ni hao?
Hello (lit., you well?)

Zaijian
Goodbye (lit., again see)

Xie xie
Thank you

Bu keqi
You're welcome (in reply to thank you)

Duibuqi
Sorry, excuse me (not used as much as in English)

Duile
Yes (lit., correct)

Shi de
Yes (lit., it is so)

Bu shi
No (lit., it is not so)

Qing zuo
Please be seated

Qing gei wo
Please give me

Qing jin
Please come in

Yingguo
England

Yingguoren
Englishman/woman

Yingyu
English (language)

Meiguo
America

Meiguoren
American man/woman

Zhongguo
China

Zhonguoren
Chinese man/woman

Hanyu (in the PRC)
Chinese (language)

Jianada
Canada

Jianadaren
Canadian

Aodaliya
Australia

Aodilayaren
Australian man/woman

Wo bu hui shuo hanyu
I can't speak Chinese

Wo shi
I am...

Zai nar
Where is...?

Sanguan
Restaurant

Fandian
Hotel

Cesuo
Toilet

Huochizhan
Railway station

Ziyou shichang
Market

Note

There are no direct equivalents for "Yes," "No," or "Please." For "Yes" you could use *duile*, which really means "correct"; or you can say, *shi de*, which means, "it is so." Instead of "No," you could sometimes use *bu shi*. As for "Please," you will hear Chinese people using *qing* followed by a verb, but this literally means "I invite you to…" For example, you can say *qing gei wo* (please give me), or *qing jin* (please come in).

Further Reading

Chinese Language
Mandarin Chinese. A Complete Course. New York: Living Language, 2005.
In-Flight Chinese. New York: Living Language, 2001.
BBC Mandarin Phrasebook. London: BBC Books, 2005.
The BBC languages Web site is useful for learning some phrases before you go, and you can download the lessons to practice on the plane:
http://www.bbc.co.uk/languages/chinese/

Background: History, Economy, Politics
Becker, Jasper. *Hungry Ghosts: Mao's Secret Famine,* London: John Murray 1996.
——— *The Chinese.* New York: Free Press, 2000.
——— *The City of Heavenly Tranquility: Beijing in the History of China.* New York, Oxford University Press USA, 2008
Harney, Alexandra. *The China Price: The True Cost of China's Competitive Advantage.* New York: The Penguin Press, 2008.
Fenby, Johnathan. *The Penguin History of Modern China: The Fall and Rise of a Great Power, 1850–2009.* London: Penguin Books, 2009.
Chang, Jung. *Wild Swans: Three Daughters of China.* London: HarperCollins, 2004.
——— *Mao, The Unknown Story .* New York: Knopf/London: Jonathan Cape, 2005.

Business
Kitto, Mark. *China Cuckoo: How I Lost a Fortune and Found a Life in China.* London: Constable & Robinson, 2009. (Published in the US under the title *Chasing China.*)
A cautionary tale from a British entrepreneur in China
Perkowski, Jack. *Managing the Dragon. How I'm Building a Billion Dollar Business in China.* New York: Random House, 2008.
Perkowski has survived thirteen years of running ASIMCO Technologies in China, and his book is full of insights.

Web Sites
http://www.danwei.org/
Web site for all things Chinese, with many useful links for businesspeople.

http://www.eiu.com/index.asp
Economist Intelligence Unit, with up-to-date analysis on all aspects of doing business in China.

http://www.thechinabeat.org/
Context and criticism on contemporary China from China scholars and journalists.

Index